THE Master Plan

THE Master Plan

Your Financial Blueprint to Building a Better Future

JONATHAN PEYTON

Printed in the United States of America

Library of Congress Control Number: 2018940107

ISBN Paperback: 978-1-947368-84-2
ISBN Hardcover: 978-1-947368-89-7
ISBN Audiobook: 978-1-947368-90-3

If you are reading this then you have already accomplished something many others have failed to do. You took the first step. A step that thousands before you have dreaded. You put something in motion that only stops if you stop…

I dedicate this book to you… because you control what happens from here… Use what you learn in this book to take control of your financial life, either on your own or with the help of a trusted advisor.
Remember, planning for a better future starts today!

Contents

Acknowledgements

To my past, present, and future clients: I would like to thank the thousands of you who have shaped my perspective on what it truly means to live a full life. I am blessed to have heard your amazing stories and be a part of your life. You continue to push me to be a student of learning, and life, so I can share more of my knowledge with each new person I meet.

To my family: You have supported me through some highs and graciously put up with me through some lows. Between working late hours, weekends, and disappearing for extended periods of time into my home office, I wouldn't be here without your support. A testament to a person's success is based on the people they surround themselves with. I am so lucky that you have kept me around this long...

Invitation

"We're too smart these days. We've grown so inured to the often unbelievable nonsense on television, or the absurd chain emails we gather in our inboxes, that the idea of a hysteria-inciting radio (*radio!*) play is laughable. So try, for a spell, to put yourself in the shoes of listeners who tuned in 70 years ago to The Mercury Theater on the Air's performance of *The War of the Worlds*."[1]

So writes Gilbert Cruz in a reflection on Orson Welles' infamous radio show, which panicked audiences across the nation misinterpreted as the frantic news announcement of an extraterrestrial invasion. Many decades have passed since then, and we laugh about it now, but the incident touches on a sensitive but true observation: sometimes, it's not so easy to separate fact from fiction. With the amount of unbelievable nonsense that circulates through the Internet, radio, and television, how does anyone determine what is real and what is hype or "fake news"?

---

1 Gilbert Cruz, "Orson Welles' *War of the Worlds*," *Time*, Oct. 30, 2008, http://content.time.com/time/arts/article/0,8599,1855120,00.html.

I am so glad you took the first step toward planning for a better future by purchasing this book. Building a better financial future is not easy and it takes a fair amount of work, but with the right elbow grease in the right place, the process can move quickly.

My name is Jonathan Peyton. I have spent over a decade helping thousands of clients assess, evaluate, prepare, and execute planning strategies to improve their financial situation, covering essential topics like budgeting, tax planning, investment strategies, estate planning, protection strategies, and much more.

I started off my career wanting to be an investment banker, but a passion for personal finance arose when I fell in love with the stories of people I talked to and the lives that they were living. When I left, I moved into financial planning with one of the "big box" financial planning firms, but I soured on that when I saw that their focus was too much on the Almighty Dollar and not enough on helping families build the lives they wanted. I knew there must be a better way. Plus, I didn't just want to work for someone else my whole life.

After some time, the stars aligned and the opportunity came for me to branch out on my own. Using my own savings, I took the leap and went into private practice, determined to make something for myself and build a business that I thought the world needed: holistic financial planning that helps people in every facet of life and works with them the way *they* want rather than having someone tell them how it should be. This multifaceted approach is rarely seen in the industry, but I've developed an entire business around the idea.

I've made it a lifelong pursuit to become knowledgeable on a broad range of subjects, rather than an expert on just one. After investing more than $100,000 in higher education, today I hold these degrees and certifications:

- A bachelor's in economics
- An executive MBA
- The CERTIFIED FINANCIAL PLANNER™ certification through the Certified Financial Planning Board of Standards
- The Certified Divorce Financial Analyst® certification through the Institute of Divorce Financial Analysts
- The Chartered Special Needs Consultant™ certification through The American College of Financial Services
- An Executive Certificate in Financial Planning from the Georgetown University School of Continuing Studies
- The Certified Product Manager & Certified Product Marketing Manager certifications through the Association of International Product Marketing & Management

That may seem like a lot, but I'm not done yet. I hold the Certified Value Growth Advisor designation and Certified Exit Planning Advisor certification to support Entrepreneurs. I believe that the more I can learn how different topics are integrated, the easier it will be to find the common threads that I can then teach to people like you.

That is the philosophy that underpins this book. Planning for the future is more than just choosing stocks for your portfolio, calculating rates of return, or taking out the right insurance. It means looking at all areas of your financial life simultaneously to prevent any weak points or blind spots.

After reading hundreds of perspectives on what financial planning includes and how investors should strategize for the future, I came to realize that most financial "advice" out there is not crafted for the consumer's benefit, but is just a way to push the author's agenda. To combat the flood of misinformation, I decided to write this book with only two goals in mind: to pull back the curtain on the financial services industry and to give you an actionable blueprint to build a comprehensive financial plan on your own, or with the guidance of a trusted advisor. It's the same blueprint I use in my wealth management practice when helping clients. This book provides you the same expertise my clients pay $400 an hour and thousands of dollars a year to receive.

My only request is that you give this book your best effort. Certain topics are challenging, but the information can be life-changing. The strategies I'll discuss have saved or made many tens of thousands of dollars for my clients over the years. Throughout the book I have provided stories from previous clients as examples. To protect their privacy I have changed all of their personally identifiable details.

This book doesn't cover every conceivable aspect of every financial topic, but it *does* provide a solid foundation for assessing, developing, and implementing a sound financial plan that will endure for years or decades—provided you conduct the necessary periodic review. It will be your job to build on this plan and tailor the information to your personal situation. In the end, you have control. No one but you can stand in the way of realizing your dreams.

CHAPTER 1

Pulling Back the Curtain

In the world of financial advice, it seems like everyone has an opinion. An opinion on how to budget your money. An opinion on what the right investment mix should be. An opinion on whether to pay off your home or leverage it to the hilt. Heck, even an opinion on what precious metal to own when modern civilization comes crashing down. Opinions may be America's most abundant natural resource.

For this, you can blame the internet, which allows anyone with a smartphone or laptop to make the world into their own personal soapbox, from which they can spread their gospel while tearing down the opinions of those who disagree. The internet has provided us with unprecedented access to knowledge—but it has also created an unfettered platform from which liars, charlatans, and scoundrels can push bad advice. Television is guilty of the same sins: the incessant twenty-four-hour broadcast means that there are twenty-four hours of talking heads who have a lot to say about your investment strategy, but they won't be the ones left holding the bag if things don't pan out. Now, these individuals aren't all bad, and sometimes they offer valuable suggestions, but they're being paid to drive ratings, not to protect your financial health.

The flood of expert and not-so-expert advice can muddy the waters and impede your ability to make prudent decisions about your financial future. How, then, do you separate the good from the bad? How do you wade through the swamp to find the right answers for your unique situation? It comes down to trust, transparency, and knowing what questions to ask and of whom to ask them. This book will teach you how to ask those questions; build a sound, all-inclusive financial plan; and protect your and your family's livelihood.

Fact versus Hype

Turn on the television and flip to any business channel, and you will find no shortage of besuited bobbleheads holding forth about a company's latest news, preaching how to invest in an ever-changing market, or sharing their hot take on the controversial politician of the day. These are the topics that drive ratings, and ratings are what drive their salaries. Many of these pundits have a background in finance or investment banking, which in the eyes of the viewer makes them qualified to speak on almost any financial topic. However, their qualification to give meaningful or actionable advice that directly impacts the everyday American stops the moment the camera starts rolling. How can we know if their words are more fact than hype when they are cashing high six- or low seven-figure checks from the broadcast networks? Is the insight they provide really designed to serve the public, or is it designed to titillate their group of followers who drink their particular brand of Kool-Aid?

2

The same came be said of the so-called gurus, people like Dave Ramsey and Suze Orman, whose legions of devotees keep them forever in the spotlight. This is not to begrudge them their success or deny that they're well-informed about the markets (though you know what they say about a stopped clock), but there is often a fine line separating "gurus" from "charlatans." And sometimes that line runs right through your balance sheet, at precisely the point that separates the black ink from the red.

The problem is not just with the televised gurus or the financial Twitterati. Even professional financial advisors with fancy titles and lofty certifications attached to their names might be doling out advice that benefits themselves first and you second. For example, many financial advisors work on a commission basis, receiving a cut from third-party products they sell to clients (i.e., life insurance policies).

Commission-based work is not inherently problematic, but it does raise the potential for conflict of interest. I have met many "financial advisors" working on a commission basis who have a handful of go-to products they know inside out and recommend to almost every client they meet with, regardless of whether these products are suited to the client's particular needs. This practice is particularly common among the "big box" investment firms, which are less focused on transparency and which sometimes take an assembly-line approach to their long and unwieldy client list. I should know—I used to be employed by a couple of those large firms. In my opinion, comprehensive advice was hit or miss, depending on the person you talked to on any given day. "One size fits all" might work well for snapback baseball caps but not so much when your livelihood is at stake.

Nothing in Life Is Free

If you close your eyes, spin around, and throw a rock in any direction, there's a good chance you'll hit someone giving away financial "advice" or "coaching" or "guidance," often for free. Many big box firms lure consumers in with free advice, only to try to sell them something on their product shelf. This low-key bait-and-switch highlights a simple truth: Nothing is ever really given away for free. There is always a cost somewhere.

Financial bloggers are another group who are giving away a "free" product. It might be free to read, but it could cost you in other ways, so take financial bloggers' advice with a grain of salt. Now, many financial bloggers are savvy, intelligent, and dedicated to providing information that is beneficial to their readership. But some bloggers are motivated by self-interest—the more clicks and page views they get, the more they profit (either from advertising dollars or subscription services). Making money from their labor isn't bad in and of itself, but unfortunately, the nature of blogging as a business incentivizes certain bad practices: the kind of clickbait, sensationalist content that drives viewers to websites may not be the kind of content that is good for your portfolio.

Moreover, financial bloggers are writing for a general audience, and their advice may not be applicable to your own individual situation. That's why you'll often find this Federal Trade Commission–mandated disclaimer at the bottom of the page: "The information contained on this website is the opinion of the individual authors based on their personal observation, research, and years of experience. The publisher and its authors are not registered investment advisers, attorneys, CPAs, or other financial service professionals and do not render legal, tax, accounting, or investment advice or other professional services. The information offered by this website is intended for general education only. Because each individual's factual situation is different, the reader should seek his or her own personal adviser. . . . Use at your own risk."

Whatever the source—whether bloggers, commission-based advisors, or others—you need to question the information you receive. It is possible that the people giving you the information are trying to help you. They could be providing valuable insight to improve your life and the lives of your loved ones. Or their motivations could be hidden, which means you might have to dig deeper into the information they give you. The more transparent people are about their intentions and motivations, the easier it will be for you to make an informed decision. And the more informed you are, the better your decision-making will be.

In the end, transparency builds trust and tells you whether those you work with have integrity. It doesn't matter if it's with your friends, family, coworkers, or even your financial planner—trust is the building block from which each relationship is forged.

Therefore, working with an advisor comes down to two principles: trust and integrity. Do you believe you can trust this person for the next ten, twenty, or thirty years? Will they be a reliable ally as you face your biggest financial fears? Are their morals aligned with yours? Do they put your interests above their own, even when doing so might lighten their wallet? If the answer to any of these questions is no, then you need to keep looking.

Name Games

In the financial services industry, financial professionals seem to cycle through titles like they are going out of style. Today they are a "financial consultant," tomorrow they could be an "insurance agent," and by Friday they're calling themselves an "asset manager." Essentially, if a financial professional feels their message isn't reaching their target audience, they can pay a little extra to obtain a certification and transform themselves into whatever they want to be. Having a title or certification alone does not make someone a great advisor.

Complicating the picture is the arcane distinction between "advis*er*" and "advis*or*," as defined by the Investment Advisers Act of 1940, which intended to crack down on abuses related to investment advice.[1] Legally, an "advis*er*" is one who provides ongoing investment advice, while an "advis*or*" is a broker who is in the business of selling various products. In practice, the term *advisor* has become synonymous with "big picture person," someone who can help with a client's insurance portfolio, retirement projections, education concerns, and a myriad of other topics. In the chart below (which measures the occurrence of the two terms in books published since 1860), we can see how the use of both words has changed over time.[2] Note the steep rise before and precipitous drop-off following the stock market crash of 1929.

To add prestige and credibility to being an advisor, the creation and use of designations has practically become a business unto itself. Today the Financial Industry Regulatory Authority (FINRA) acknowledges over 150 professional designations and certifications.[3] Yet the

---

1 Michael Kitces, "Financial Adviser vs. Advisor - What's the Difference?" *Nerd's Eye View* (blog), August 18, 2016, https://www.kitces.com/blog/financial-adviser-vs-advisor-vs-financial-planner-whats-the-difference/.

2 "Financial Adviser and Financial Advisor," Google Books Ngram Viewer, https://books.google.com/ngrams/graph?content=financial+advisor%2Cfinancial+adviser&year_start=1850&year_end=2017&corpus=15&smoothing=5&share=&direct_url=t1%3B%2Cfinancial%20advisor%3B%2Cc0%3B.t1%3B%2Cfinancial%20adviser%3B%2Cc0.

3 "Professional Designations," Financial Industry Regulatory Authority (FINRA), https://www.finra.org/investors/professional-designations.

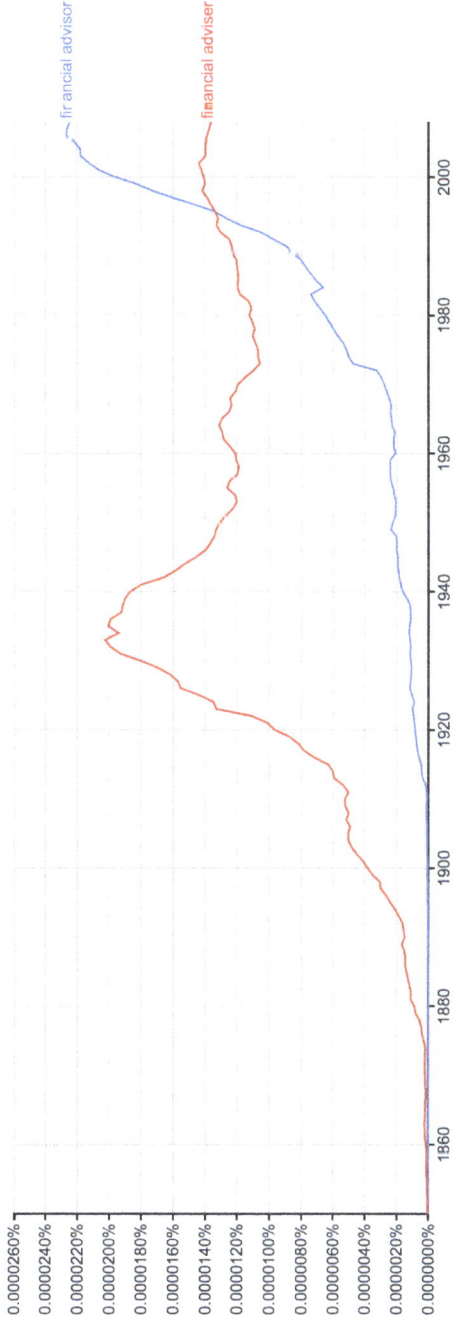

Securities and Exchange Commission (SEC) does not acknowledge any professional titles.[4] Financial professionals who sell financial products are registered with FINRA. But if you are an investment advis*er* who provides ongoing investment management, then the SEC has jurisdiction over you. It's enough to make a consumer's head spin, when the only question that really matters is this: Whom do you receive advice from today, a salesperson or an adviser? And do they have your best interest at heart?

Now let's make something clear. It is perfectly acceptable to work with both an advis*or* and an advis*er*. For some consumers, this approach could be an efficient division of labor. One person manages your portfolio while the other administers your estate planning or solves other problems. But if someone claims to be a retirement specialist or an accredited investment whatever, they should be able to explain what they do, the typical client they serve, why their process is different from their competitor's down the street, and, most importantly, how working with them will assuage your biggest financial fears. Above all, their process should not be a one-size-fits-all approach.

Having an advisor look at just your retirement picture, or investment plan, or health-care concerns to the exclusion of other areas is very shortsighted. Did they determine the tax impact of holding certain investments in one account versus another? What about how to prioritize where your excess cash flow should go to address multiple financial goals? There are so many competing issues that excluding any from the bigger picture could harm your long-term plan.

---

4 Securities and Exchange Commission (SEC), "Making Sense of Professional Financial Titles," SEC Pub. No. 160 (9/13), https://www.sec.gov/files/ib_making_sense.pdf.

Not All Plans Are Created Equal

Over the last few decades, I believe the concept of a "financial advisor" has become blurry. Who exactly is supposed to be your financial advisor? Your accountant? Your insurance agent? The guy or gal at the big box firm? Can you have multiple advisors? What happens when one specialist's advice conflicts with that of another? Or what if *you* are the one who has to stitch together a patchwork of information from different sources into a coherent plan? It may seem advantageous to have several people on your team, but the adage "two heads are better than one" can easily become a two-headed (or five-headed) monster—and each head will surely be quite vocal in telling you why his or her advice is best and the other advisors are wrong. So how do you make good choices?

You can't really count on the big box firms because most financial plans they provide are too narrowly focused and tend to address a limited portion of your financial life, like retirement or your investment mix. Making good choices starts with understanding that financial planning is a complex, multifaceted process involving financial statement preparation and analysis, insurance planning and risk management, investment planning, income tax planning, retirement planning, and estate planning. Then you need to flip through your most recent "plan" and ask yourself what kind of advice you have previously received. Determine if someone pitched you a retirement plan as a financial plan. Did you receive an investment analysis and think, "I am on the right track!"? If so, what about the other financial planning subject areas that could derail your plan? The questions can pile up quickly until they overwhelm you, leaving you in need of professional help. What then? Should you hire an advisor to manage all your advisors? You can see how the situation can quickly spin out of control.

The Master Plan

This book provides the solution: a blueprint for handling the multitude of steps needed to integrate each financial planning subject area of your life without paying thousands of dollars to someone like me to do it for you. It draws on lessons I've learned from helping thousands of people like you, and it will empower you to take control of your financial future.

As you go through this book, I want you to feel as though I have pulled you aside, sat down with you in your living room, and am telling you the secrets I've accrued throughout the last fifteen years in the profession. Reading this book will open your eyes to what the financial services industry is not telling you, while providing you with a straightforward, concrete action plan to assess the following:

1. Your current financial situation
2. Your short-term, intermediate, and long-term goals
3. Your insurance coverages and how they relate to your goals
4. Your overall investment strategy and how to build an investment plan to achieve your goals
5. Your current and future tax planning needs
6. Your legacy plans and how to address your family's financial needs in the face of a catastrophic event
7. Special circumstances that may arise, such as divorce and caring for a special needs child

The blueprint in this book is my gift to you. It can be used by someone who wants to plan their future on their own (a "doer") *or* the person who wants a benchmark for how to evaluate the advisor who handles their day-to-day operations (a "delegator"). I'll explain how these two strategies—doing and delegating—are not mutually exclusive but can be applied selectively to different aspects of your plan in a way that accords with your abilities, wants, and needs.

By the end of the book, you will be able to assess your situation, determine if you are primarily a "doer" or a "delegator," and take action by building a foundational plan for you and your loved ones—one that is durable, comprehensive, and capable of weathering the ups and downs that life will inevitably throw your way.

CHAPTER 2

Dirty Little Secrets

Whenever I meet with a new client, I make it a point to learn as much about their situation, their background, and their goals as possible. The dialogue goes both ways: the client also interviews me to make sure I am credible, knowledgeable, and truly understand their situation. This consultative interview style allows both of us to make sure there is a good fit before investing too much time and money into the financial planning process.

About three years ago I met a wonderful couple who were very interested in saving for their future but were unsure if they were doing everything they could to build a foundation. The husband was a lawyer and the wife was a doctor. They had started saving later in life after paying off some debt, and now they wanted to provide a good life for their two school-age children and build a nest egg for themselves.

At the start of the meeting, they surprised me by explaining that their previous advisor was "anti-stock market" and felt there were better options to grow *and* protect their investments without direct stock market exposure. They handed me a list of their investments and asked whether I agreed that having close to 80 percent of their investments in annuities was a sound strategy. You don't have to be a financial genius to say, "Hell no! That is not okay!" Annuities can be a valuable part of a balanced portfolio, but an 80 percent allocation to an illiquid retirement asset for two young professionals with kids was unlikely to meet their short, intermediate, and long-term goals. Additionally, they were frustrated that the performance of their annuities was lagging behind the market as a whole due to the higher internal fees and moderate risk profile.

This couple wanted market growth but also wanted principal preservation, the holy grail of any investor. To provide them with a solution, their previous advisor had told them that insurance companies offer annuities with various "guarantees" that attempt to provide more portfolio stability, market-like returns, and the opportunity for predictable income in retirement. When I asked them if they were aware how much their advisor was paid for investing $500,000 into the annuities, they, of course, had no idea.

Moreover, what was left out of the conversation, or perhaps forgotten by the clients, were the fees. On average, an annuity's total annual fees, with living benefits, can range from 1.5 percent to 3 percent, depending on the bells and whistles included.[1] Furthermore, when they decided to take some money out of the accounts for a vacation home down payment, they were hit with a bevy of unexpected penalties, fees, and taxes on the growth.

---

1 "Why Are Annuity Fees So High?," *Money*, http://time.com/money/collection-post/2791254/why-are-annuity-fees-so-high/

It was not until after they hired me that I read through the three different prospectuses and uncovered the underlying annual fees, investment rationale, and the primary purpose of these annuities. In our second meeting, I explained to the couple that their particular annuities carried a higher internal expense due to additional riders they requested. Basically, my new clients' entire plan for the future was stymied by a complete mismatch between their goals and the savings plan set up by their former advisor.

My two well-intentioned clients are hardly the only ones who have found themselves in such a predicament. It is just one of numerous cases I've seen of how even savvy, intelligent people can get lost in the morass of information and options in an industry that all too often serves itself first and customers second. But knowledge is your best defense. Protect yourself by pulling back the curtain and looking at the "dirty secrets" the industry tries to keep concealed.

Secret #1: How Advisors Get Paid

Compensation for advisors usually falls into one of three categories: 1) fee only, 2) fee-based, and 3) commission—and these three camps have been fighting a protracted war with each other over which arrangement is superior.

Fee Only

Today's debate over the different types of advisors has its origin in the 1970s and early 1980s, which were something of a Wild West era in finance, when regulations were more lax than they are today. Fewer regulations meant investment firms could charge higher loads and ticket charges on products, brokers did not have to worry about fiduciary standards, and repercussions for unscrupulous actions were limited.

In 1983, a group of advis*ors* got together to determine how they could work with clients without being compensated through commissions. It was their belief that clients would be best served in a capacity free of conflicts of interest, much like an accountant or attorney, by charging for their time rather than for the products they recommended.[2] These advisors were the first to form what is now the National Association of Personal Financial Advisors (NAPFA). NAPFA members can only sell their services on a fee-only basis.

Fee-only advisors are paid directly by the client through an hourly fee, flat fee, or as a percentage of someone's investments. They are not compensated in any other way than by the client. Such advisors insist that this approach shields them from conflicts of interest that, they allege, afflict fee-based and commission advisors, who receive a commission from financial products they sell. Fee-only advisors believe a conflict of interest arises because the advisor's compensation is tied to how many extra products the client purchases. It creates an incentive to push products with a higher fee.

Depending on the advisor's experience, the fee-only advisor may charge between $75 and $400 per hour. Flat-fee arrangements are harder to come by because they require the advisor to assess the scope of work upfront and then estimate a price. In some cases, the work may end up taking much longer than originally expected and the flat-fee arrangement becomes unprofitable to the advisor. Consequently, the advisor may overcompensate for this risk by erring on the side of charging too much rather than too little. It is not uncommon to see financial professionals charge $2,500 to

2 "History of NAPFA," National Association of Personal Financial Advisors (NAPFA), https://www.napfa.org/napfa-history

$25,000, depending on the complexity and scope of work, for a flat-fee arrangement.

While there is some merit to the fee-only camp's argument that its compensation schemes avoid conflict of interest, it doesn't address certain drawbacks of that approach. For example, when a fee-only advisor provides a financial plan without specific, actionable recommendations for investment, insurance, or other, then they are essentially leaving the client to research solutions on their own. Furthermore, the client may still need to buy commission-based financial products to implement the plan.

Moreover, there are certain advantages to working with an advisor who recommends products (whether or not he gets a cut). If I'm a fee-only advisor and I give my clients a financial plan and tell them to go and execute it on their own, how is the client supposed to discern where to go, whom to speak to, and how to shop the best type of products or services on the market? In fact, it would seem wrong for a fee-only advisor to turn a complicated financial plan over to the client without specific recommendations on where to go and what to purchase.

Unfortunately, because the fee-only advisors are not licensed with different product providers, they tend to be less well-informed on the specific nuances of various products that are needed to implement a client's financial plan. Taking a flat fee or hourly compensation for a project and then turning the client loose to fend for himself in the wilds of the financial industry is hardly a virtuous way of doing business.

Fee-Based

There is another approach, besides hourly and project-based rates, called "assets under management" (AUM). In many cases, financial professionals realize hourly and flat-fee arrangements do not generate ongoing revenue to their company, so they adopt a model where they will only work with a client who transfers a minimum amount of capital to them.

Under this arrangement, all ancillary services, like financial planning, are offered free of charge, but once the company receives the money, they charge an annual fee based on a percentage of the assets under their management. For example, if you transfer $500,000 to the company, the company could charge you 1 percent annually for ongoing investment management. This would mean you pay this company $5,000 per year. That might sound like a lot, especially because their goal should be to outpace their custom benchmarks *and* average a return that is commensurate with your financial plan's required return (after fees).

It should be said that, in my experience, this advisor's primary motivation is to manage your assets and less about financial planning or other ancillary services. Often, advisors may provide a financial review at the onset of the engagement but the ongoing reviews tend to be centered around the investments rather than the comprehensive package. Therefore, clients tend to judge the relationship based on investment performance and less on equally essential maters such as tax, estate, retirement, or other services. I call this dying on the performance sword.

Commissions: Is the Stigma Deserved?

The third group, who are compensated from commissions, typically do very little project-based work. Their compensation is primarily derived from selling. As commissioned advisors, it is their job to eat what they kill.

"Commissions" has become a dirty word in the financial services industry. But most of the people I have spoken with over the last fifteen years either do not want to know what their advisor is being paid or frankly do not care. So the real question to ask yourself is this: Which is better? Is not knowing what you are paying for on the back end better than knowing what you are paying for on the front end?

There is a solution that would help obviate commission-based advisors' potential conflict of interest, and that is simply to make commission work more transparent. This would mean commission advisors would reveal the actual commissions that the issuing company is going to pay the advisor. There is no reason why the client should not be told a product pays a 3 percent fee to the advisor for placing business with a particular company. If the benefits of the product truly outweigh anything else and will serve the client's best interest, why should the advisor be afraid to share what they are paid? To sell you the highest commission-based product, the advisor needs to disclose a lot of information about the product and the suitability of the product for your particular situation. Requiring that the advisor put all his cards on the table helps mitigate the risk of unscrupulous advice.

You may be wondering why, if you are able to build an entire comprehensive financial plan on your own and manage your investments on your own, you can't also earn a commission from financial products you purchase yourself. The reason is that every provider who creates a financial product has to make sure the people selling the product are appropriately trained on the product and trained to the standard of the regulating body that governs the provider. Therefore, in order to compensate the person for all the training they have to do and to incentivize the advisor to sell the product, the provider pays a commission for selling the product.

Whatever your belief, the best practice as the client is for you to ask your advisor if they receive commissions *and* whether or not (note the *or*) they will disclose those commissions to you *before* you purchase an investment. If they are truly transparent and want to dispel the myth that advisors working on commission are inherently less trustworthy, then they should be fine with telling you what their commission will be. Then you can make an informed decision and determine whether the advice you are receiving along with the product is worth the fee they are going to receive. If you knew that you invested $500,000 into a commission-based product and the advisor was going to receive $15,000 to $30,000 in commissions, you might make sure you completely understood everything you were about to purchase *before* purchasing it.

Asking questions will help you navigate these thorny issues and guide your decision about who will oversee your investment decisions and other important financial concerns. In subsequent chapters, I'll tell you how to ask those questions, which are the building blocks of trust and transparency.

TIP

I have noticed a rise in the number of people who provide "financial coaching." They do not claim to be advisors, but rather state that they provide financial education, coaching, or consulting. Like the bloggers and on-air personalities, many of these people operate under the FTC's regulatory direction instead of the SEC's or FINRA's financial regulatory guidelines. This distinction is very important because there is a significant difference in the kind of guidance they can provide, the laws that they have to follow, and the penalties that can befall them. For example, they are not bound to fiduciary or suitability standards, which we will discuss later. Many are not trained in some of the personal and business complexities, or strategies, that tenured advisors with specialized degrees or certifications are required to maintain continuing education in. There is nothing that prevents them from putting their interests above yours throughout the duration of the relationship.

A way to know you are working with someone like this is when they use testimonials in their marketing. If they were regulated by the SEC, then they would be prohibited from using testimonials in digital or printed marketing materials pursuant to Rule 206(4)-1(a)(1).[3] If you decide to work with someone like this please make sure you understand their business, their legal requirements, the type of coaching they are allowed to provide, and the rules that protect you if the worst were to occur.

Secret #2: Big Box versus Independent Firms

The classic David and Goliath struggle rages on in the financial services industry: the scrappy "little guy" pitted against the tyranny of the bigger regime. This is how I feel when I try to fight against the companies who have more money, a larger legal team, and more marketing prowess.

---

3 "Guidance on the Testimonial Rule and Social Media," US Securities and Exchange Commission, Accessed February 19, 2018: https://www.sec.gov/investment/im-guidance-2014-04.pdf

There is a lot to be said for having a massive war chest to market to a target audience. In the financial services industry it seems like there is a race to zero in trading fees and a race to increase the "share of wallet" each company quantifies their investors by. I once worked for a firm whose primary business model was based on trading research and trading fees. They wanted to provide high quality research to lure investors in and offer them extremely competitive trading fees in order to get them to trade on their platform. But the research and trading fees were just bait for other products they offered.

The firm knew that on average, for every person who had a trading account, they could sell a specific number of other products that would bring in extra revenue. Furthermore, each "add-on" sale did not cost the company any additional advertising money, as they were selling to an existing client. When successful, this "trade bait" gimmick helped drive customer acquisition costs down quite significantly, since the free stuff (the high quality research and so forth) eventually paid for itself.

To increase the customer's share of wallet, many of the big investment firms dangle a free financial review or diagnosis with the expectation that the results will put the financial professional in a position to pitch other products on the company's shelf. For example, you complete a retirement analysis and find you are deficient in one or two areas. "How do I fill this gap?" you ask yourself. Naturally, you consult the financial professional, who conveniently says, "Well, Mr. and Mrs. Jones, in order to get you back on track, you should consider the following . . ."

The professional usually does not explain that they will be recommending only one of the products on their shelf. If there were a better product at a different company with lower fees that would more adequately support your long-term goals, they cannot recommend it. Why? This is what is called "selling away." Essentially it is the company's way of making sure their employees only sell what is on their shelf.

If someone is offering you something for free, you should proceed with caution. Maybe that sounds cynical, but I have worked for such firms and was told to give clients free retirement income plans toutat I knew would only reveal part of the clients' overall picture. Of course I made sure to provide them with more than the bare minimum, but other advisors were not as altruistic.

If you see a financial professional for retirement advice, they will help you look at your stopgap needs for retirement and whether your investment allocation is appropriately balanced to yield the return needed to achieve your retirement goals at the time the analysis is run.

However, there are a couple of extremely eye-opening points to consider here. First, the analysis is based on today. Unless you go back periodically throughout the year, every year, your retirement strategy could drift off track. Second, the retirement analysis looks at cash flow needs, your current balance sheet, how much you are saving, and how your portfolio is invested. What about all of the other obstacles that could prevent you from reaching your goal? For example, what happens if you want to buy a home, send a kid to college, become disabled, adopt more children, or end up needing to financially support family?

The list can go on and on. You must consider a litany of external objectives and risks that could prevent you from reaching your target return. If you are not building an overall financial plan and then determining what your required investment return should be to achieve *all* of your goals, how accurate is your financial picture?

The big box advisors tend to overlook these points because with them, you are not so much a person as a number in the database. They might tell you that you are a valued client who is cultivating a professional relationship with "your guy or gal," but ask your advisor how many other people they work with. When I first started in the financial services industry, many of the senior advisors were working with 750 to 1,000 households with an average net worth ranging from $50,000 to $5 million.

Let's do the math. If your advisor works with 500 households and he promises to meet with all of them two to four times a year (so, an average of three), that's 1,500 meetings each year. Assume there are 260 working calendar days in any given year and subtract 14 days for holidays and vacation and another 7 days for personal or sick time. That leaves 239 working days. Now divide 1,500 meetings into 239 working days and your advisor holds 6.27 meetings per day. If a meeting lasts seventy-five minutes on average, then they are working almost eight hours a day. This time does not include administrative tasks, investment research, returning calls or emails, eating, or even going to the bathroom.

Therefore, the probability that all 500 households are being served equally is slim. So who do you think receives more of your advisor's attention? Exactly—the clients generating more revenue.

So where does that leave you? Let's see if we can paint a picture. You are a busy person. You decided you needed some help but were not sure if paying someone for advice was worth it. Instead you went to a big box firm where they offered free financial guidance. They provided a nice printout pamphlet that told you whether you were on track for retirement and if your asset allocation was correctly aligned with your long-term goals. Unfortunately, they left out other competing goals, such as whether you had the correct insurance policies in place to protect your home, life, and income—but OK, that wasn't why you went there in the first place.

When they gave you their pretty analysis, they suggested some changes in order to keep you on track for retirement. You asked them what you should do and they conveniently told you either to do your own research, since you were self-directed, or that they could do it for you. Again, while you are an intelligent, financially savvy person, you do not have the skill, will, or time to initiate your own action. Therefore, you turn to the professional and tell them to do it for you. You sign on the dotted line and walk out, pleased that you took an important step toward securing your future.

But a couple of months go by and you haven't really heard anything from "your guy." You ask what the process for working together will look like and want to know how often you will be able to meet to obtain progress updates. This is where knowing the right questions to ask the advisor can help uncover hidden truths, like the fact that your $500,000, while a lot to you, doesn't even put you in the top 25 percent of his clientele. I'll talk more about this in chapter 10.

More time goes by and you find that you're only getting updates once a year, if not every other year. Maybe regular meetings are not important to you, but let me ask this: How often do you have your car serviced in a given year? A car is a depreciating asset that you have to replace every seven to ten years, if not sooner, if you lease. So why do you see your mechanic more often than you see your financial professional? In the end, ask yourself, "How 'free' was the big box firm's advice, and what am I giving up by not being more actively involved in the entire financial planning process?"

Secret #3: Hidden Standards (Fiduciary versus Suitability)

You might think that the law would hold advisors to the highest professional standard—or at least, mandate that they do what's best for the client, even when it's not necessarily best for the advisor. But that isn't quite the case. This is, in general terms, the distinction between "fiduciary" and "suitability"—and the distinction is not a mere technicality, but rather one that has major implications for your financial well-being.

In 2016, the Department of Labor issued a rule (the "fiduciary rule") stipulating that an advisor assisting clients with their retirement accounts must put the interests of the client above all else when making investment recommendations. Note that the rule stipulated "retirement" accounts, not all accounts. To be classified as a fiduciary requires a more stringent standard of accountability than suitability, legally requiring advisors to prioritize the client's interest rather than just presenting "suitable" investments. The fiduciary standard also mandates a higher level of transparency for disclosing conflicts of interest. Under the suitability standard, which is less apt to put the customer first, advisors have more leeway to put their, or their company's, interests ahead of the client.

Since the announcement of the fiduciary rule, companies have been scrambling to create, train, and monitor how their advisors work with client retirement accounts. Acting in a fiduciary capacity imposes stricter requirements to make sure clients are best served. Fortunately for advisors everywhere, and unfortunately for those at NAPFA (which has long boasted of its *fiduciary* distinction), any advisor who works with retirement accounts is required to act in a fiduciary capacity. This rule is a win for investors everywhere and a huge blow to the exclusivity that organizations like NAPFA have held for so many years. That is, unless the government decides to overturn this regulation, as they've done with other investor-friendly rules.

Beyond the specifics of the rule itself, the issue raises a different question that everyone really should think about. Why did it take a government entity to step in and address the fears and concerns of the American people about being taken advantage of rather than the industry setting its own standards for how advisors should work with client retirement accounts? This just underscores the fact that the industry often serves itself first and the public second.

If you're still confused about the difference between fiduciary and suitability, consider the following situation. Imagine you've arrived at the office in the morning and find that you're rather thirsty after a longer-than-usual commute. In the lobby is a snack cart that sells coffee and water. The coffee is a dollar and the water is ten cents. As you stand in line, you consider how to quench your thirst.

The guy behind the counter asks you what you want, and you respond, "I don't know, I am here because . . . and I am looking for . . ." Of course, the guy has seen this dazed look before, so he starts to spout off some options, replete with technical jargon about the different types of coffee, where they were cultivated, and how they're brewed, before eventually ending with, "Oh, and we have water too."

Coffee has a much stronger taste than water, has short-term perks (thanks to caffeine), does not rehydrate you as adequately, costs ten times as much, and ultimately still leaves you feeling thirsty. If the cart attendant had bothered to ask you questions about your upcoming day, whether you were an avid coffee drinker, or even about why you stopped at his cart in the first place, he might have uncovered more information that could have resulted in you choosing water over coffee.

Was the higher commission of coffee over water driving his recommendation? Did he put your interest above his own? Had he been acting in a fiduciary capacity and dug deeper, he might have recommended five cups of water at a fraction of the cost, which would have carried you through lunch, versus the one cup of coffee (which you will finish by the end of the board meeting). Therein lies the true challenge of making a "suitable" as opposed to "fiduciary" investment recommendation.

CHAPTER 3

Self-Assessment: Gut-Check Time

It was winter. The year was coming to a close. While everyone around me was winding down for the holidays, I was in the throes of year-end planning. Between Thanksgiving and New Year's Eve, I am usually in back-to-back meetings. When everyone is off, they want to meet, and what better time than the end of the year?

This holiday season was shaping up to be like every other year. However, this time, there was a new couple who wanted to come in because the husband was hoping to retire by the end of the year and they were not sure if they could afford it.

Our first meeting started out like most of my meetings, where we exchanged questions and talked about their situation and expectations. The husband explained he was planning to retire at sixty while his wife, who was a few years younger, would continue to work. He stated that he had been employed since he was fifteen years old and was mentally done with work. When I asked him what he wanted to do in his retirement years, he laid out all the activities he intended to do, how he would spend his days on the golf course and take lavish trips to far-flung locales.

After the husband articulated his retirement vision, I turned to his wife and asked her what her plans for retirement were. Bemused, she said she hadn't given much thought to it because she was younger and felt retirement was seven to ten years away. I told her our goal would then be to spend the next few years helping her create a vision for her post-work life as she approached her target retirement date. It was then that she stated she didn't really have a target retirement date because she didn't know if she could afford to stop working since her husband had some pretty lofty retirement goals. This was the light-bulb moment that led to a very in-depth discussion about how much their joint retirement picture would cost.

Throughout the next three meetings, we talked through how much they had saved, how much income was coming in versus going out monthly, and where they saw themselves spending their money. It became abundantly clear that neither of them had given much thought to their spending patterns during their working years and how their preretirement spending would impact funding their retirement goals.

This situation is more common than I would prefer to see. Often, it's those just starting out in life and those nearing retirement who are least likely to have a firm understanding of what they spend their money on or what are their goals for the future. This is why assessing where you are in relation to where you want to be is vital in determining your future success. This chapter teaches you how to assess your situation using the same questions and tactics I use with my clients.

The Balance Sheet

If you have spent any time in business, you know what a corporate balance sheet looks like, and this section will be a high-level overview.

However, if your professional path has led you down a different field and into a career of service, government work, or maybe something more hands-on, then let me explain the importance of a balance sheet.

When you go for a medical checkup, the doctor assesses your current medical state by poking and prodding you to determine your overall physical health. Well, a balance sheet is much the same approach, but without the backless gown or the poking. A balance sheet is a list of the following:

1. Current assets
2. Long-term assets
3. Current liabilities (short-term debts)
4. Long-term liabilities (long-term debts)
5. Personal use assets

Current assets can be classified as something you own and that can be liquidated, or sold, within twelve months without penalties, major fees, or a large impact on value. Similarly, current liabilities are debts you intend to pay off over the next twelve months.

For example, if you have $10,000 in your checking account, that would be a current asset, whereas an employer retirement plan, like a 401(k), might not be accessible within twelve months without fees, penalties, or taxes.

An example of a current liability is the payments you make on your car over the next twelve months. If you owe $15,000 on your car and your monthly payment is $300 per month, then $300 per month multiplied by twelve months is $3,600 paid toward that loan over those twelve months (assuming a 0 percent interest rate). The $3,600 is classified as a current liability.

Long-term assets and liabilities are treated in much the same way but are valued as something that will be held longer than twelve months. You would classify your employer-sponsored retirement plan as a long-term asset, for example, since it is used to fund retirement. In the case of long-term liabilities, we would classify the remaining portion of the car loan as a long-term liability. Therefore, at the time you prepare your balance sheet, you would subtract $3,600 from $15,000 to arrive at $11,400 in long-term liabilities. When you update your balance sheet annually, you adjust the long-term liabilities amount by what you paid off over the prior year.

Personal use assets are assets that you use in daily living. A range of things fall under this category, but for sake of simplicity, we are going to consider personal use assets as your furniture, your jewelry, your electronics, your collectibles, and anything else you did not list in the current or long-term asset category.

One of the purposes of putting a balance sheet together is to determine your overall financial health. This becomes especially important in the event of a catastrophe. In other words, if something tragic were to happen and you needed cash quickly, what could you sell so that you could weather that tragedy? Having an inventory of all your assets means you know exactly what you have and where you need to go if you need to pay for an emergency.

To gauge the general health of your finances, we can quickly subtract your liabilities from your assets and arrive at your net worth. A positive net worth is the equivalent of a thumbs-up from your doctor. The opposite can be said about a negative net worth. However, just as your health can change over time, so can your net worth. Therefore, you need to constantly monitor your financial health. Below is an example of a balance sheet:

Balance Sheet					
Current Asset(s)			Current Liabilities		
	Balance				Balance
Checking	$2,000		Credit Card(s)		$2,250
Savings	$5,000		Braces		$2,000
Certificate of Deposit	$7,500		Home Loan		$17,250
Subtotal	$14,500		Boat Loan		$2,400
			Car Loan		$7,500
Long-Term Asset(s)			Subtotal		$31,400
Home**	$250,000		Long-Term Liabilities		
Boat**	$15,000				
Car**	$12,000		Home Loan		$186,000
Retirement Plan	$123,000		Boat Loan		$9,000
Subtotal	$400,000		Car Loan		$15,000
			Subtotal		$210,000
Personal Use Asset(s)					
			Total Liabilities		$241,400
Jewelry	$6,000				
Electronics	$4,000		Total Assets		$429,500
Furniture	$5,000		Total Liabilities		$241,400
Subtotal	$15,000		Net Worth		$188,100
Total Assets	$429,500				
***A home, car, and a boat can also be classified as personal use assets. This is subject to your classification.					

33

The above illustration is a simplified version of a balance sheet; yours could be much more complicated. Without knowing your financial health before making a major life decision like having children, purchasing a house, or retiring, then you could be setting yourself up for some serious financial hardship.

Now let's talk about how your monthly budget can affect your balance sheet.

Cash Flow (Budget)

If you thought preparing a balance sheet was complicated, building a cash flow statement is easy by comparison. For the purpose of this book, let's call a cash flow statement a "budget." Companies prepare cash flow statements as a second method of gauging their financial health and determining ongoing profitability. Similar to how corporate America uses a cash flow statement, the average American can use a budget to track the following:

1. What their money is spent on
2. Whether they are overspending
3. How future purchases will be paid for
4. Whether they are contributing enough to their future goals

Each of these points will become integral to increasing your net worth and funding your goals. Unless you know where your money goes, how will you know if you have enough to finance a car, purchase a home, send your child to college, or save for retirement? However, if it's so essential, then why do households fail to use a budget? In my experience there are two reasons: being overly busy or laziness.

How many times have you started a workweek, blinked, and found yourself turning off the lights as you were leaving the office on Friday evening? Where does the time go? Between daily responsibilities at work, taking care of the kids, and maybe some social life, people tend to place managing their finances lower on the priority list. I cannot tell you how many times I have looked at my own bills at the end of the month and said, "I spent how much?" Before I built my system, I could go an entire month without looking at my bank balance once, all the while praying I was not overspending. After all, we're all only human. (Yes, even us financial advisors, contrary to popular belief.)

I have found that most Americans don't really think closely about their cash flow beyond the general rule of "try to spend less than we bring in." When we overspend, we find ourselves having to dip into other accounts, or carry a balance on credit cards. When we spend less than we bring in, the surplus usually sits in a checking or savings account until we have enough time to figure out where else to put the leftover money. Unfortunately, this mindset is very "in the moment" and does not work well when planning for future or for unforeseen events. Living in the moment can leave you unprepared for the future, sometimes with disastrous consequences.

Now that we've talked about the value of creating and, more importantly, maintaining a budget, let's get to the important stuff: how to actually do it. The first step is choosing which system you will use. Some people love Excel spreadsheets, while others do not even know how to use one. As technology has advanced, companies have created a variety of tools (online, for your PC, and for mobile) that allow you to build, monitor, and manage your budget daily. In my experience, many of these tools are nice on the outside but lack integration with other areas of your financial life.

For example, a popular app many people use is called Mint. When I used it in the early 2000s, I found all Mint could do was aggregate data feeds from all of my external accounts like my credit cards, mortgage, and car loans. Once the data was aggregated, I could devise a budget inside Mint based on the categories I created and determine if I was staying within my monthly budget. What the budgeting tool did not do was, for example, tell me how cutting my expenses by $100 per month would accelerate saving for my daughter's education by an additional year or two.

For this reason, I decided to go back to the trusted pencil-and-paper method. This way I could easily manipulate the numbers and determine how cutting my entertainment budget by $100 per month would affect other areas of my life. Eventually, I returned to a digital method of budgeting, and now I use software that integrates my outside accounts in one place and allows me to create, monitor, and manage my budget, and determine how tweaking it can accelerate meeting my other goals. This is the same software I use in daily practice with my clients. They use it so both they and I can stay on top of their financial life now *and* stay on top of their future goals. This proprietary tool turns managing finances—a task that took an hour or two per week—into a fifteen to twenty minute task on a Saturday morning over a cup of coffee.

The bottom line: find a process that works for you. Just because an app is popular or user-friendly does not make it a panacea for all of your budgetary needs. A good tool will integrate multiple areas of your financial life and allow you to spend more time with your loved ones rather than on the unpleasant process of number crunching.

Now that we have talked about how having a budget can benefit you today and how it can be used to plan for the future, I want to show you how easy it is to create one.

Monthly Summary By Category			
Income			
Spouse 1 Net Salary	$3,250.00		
Spouse 2 Net Salary	$3,400.00		
Total	$6,650.00		
Category	Budget	Actual	Difference
Auto	$200.00	$198.00	$2.00
Gas	$75.00	$64.00	$11.00
Entertainment	$200.00	$400.00	($200.00)
Food	$350.00	$205.75	$144.25
Home	$1,250.00	$1,250.00	$0.00
Cell Phone	$100.00	$97.00	$3.00
Personal Items	$300.00	$120.00	$180.00
Kids	$200.00	$350.00	($150.00)
Utilities	$200.00	$175.00	$25.00
Other	$50.00	$60.00	($10.00)
Total	$2,925.00	$2,919.75	$5.25
Surplus/Deficit (Net Budget)	$3,725.00	$2,919.75	$805.25

A simple spreadsheet or pencil and paper can give you a pretty deep understanding of what your priorities are and where you should refocus them. If you find yourself with a few extra dollars at the end of each month (like the $805.25 in the previous example), you can begin redirecting those dollars to another account that is tied to a specific goal like college, a house purchase, or retirement. On the other hand, if you find yourself with a negative amount at the end of each month, then you need to reevaluate where that money is going and determine if you can reduce expenses somewhere. If you look at your budget and realize you cannot reduce your expenses, then the only way to turn a negative budget into a positive one is to increase your income, which will require reevaluating your employment situation. My suggestion is to consider paring down expenses, which is usually more feasible than finding alternative employment or taking on a second job.

TIP

Operating your household on a budget, regardless of your income, will help you understand where your money goes. If you are scraping by, then a budget will help you better prioritize your current and future goals. On the other hand, if you have a large surplus of income, a budget will help you determine if you are optimizing where you contribute the excess cash flow. A budget can make your money go farther and work harder, which could yield higher returns depending on where you save or invest any surplus.

Goal Statement

Now that we have laid the foundation for the balance sheet and the budget, we turn our attention to the goal statement. This one might sound simple, but it is one of the hardest tasks to complete. Why? Well, it requires you to think outside of the box and dream. But wait, why is dreaming so hard? Answer this: How many of you know exactly where your next vacation will be, or what college your child will attend, or if you will still be living where you currently reside when you retire?

In most cases, when I ask clients for a goal statement, they give me a few lines of hypothetical goals but the details are sort of fuzzy. The when, where, how long, and how much are rough estimates, at best. Too often we are focused on what is in front of us and think less about what will happen years from now. This is where some outside help may be needed. I always encourage clients to talk with friends, relatives, neighbors, and coworkers about where they go and what they are planning for.

I even tell my clients to head over to their local Barnes & Noble to check out the magazine section. Growing up, I hated books, which is ironic now that I'm writing one, but I loved the magazine section. There are so many interesting topics, hobbies, and travel magazines that there are bound to be at least one or two publications that spark interest. If you're looking for direction, that interest is what will help you begin to build your goal statement and map out what you are planning for.

Once you know where you are planning to go or what you want to save for, you can begin working backwards with your budget and balance sheet to determine how long it will take you to save for that particular goal. It is important to note that I said "save," not "charge it." According to the Center of Macroeconomic Data at the Federal Reserve, in the first quarter of 2017, the average American household carried over $6,000 in credit card debt. However, when you cut out the households that do not carry a recurring credit card balance month to month, the average balance for the 48 million households that do carry credit card debt jumps to over $15,000 per household.[1]

---

1 Brittany Meyer, "2017 Statistics Show Average Credit Card Debt Rising in American Households," BadCredit.org, July 28, 2017, http://www.badcredit.org/studies/average-credit-card/

Achieving future goals with mounting debt becomes nearly impossible when the debt collectors inevitably come knocking.

When building a goal statement, you want to break it into three parts. The first part will outline goals in the "short term," which I define as zero to five years. A goal in this time frame has high priority and will most likely require allocation of resources from the balance sheet. Additionally, within this time frame you need to prioritize your goals in case you do not have the resources to accomplish all of them. Prioritization allows you to determine how much of your wish list is actually achievable in any time period.

The second part of your goal statement will be broken down into intermediate goals of between six and fifteen years. This window of time is just enough that you can consider directing a larger portion of your monthly savings toward intermediate goals. The shorter end of the list may require tapping into your balance sheet, but depending on how lofty the goals are, your cash flow should be able to meet a large portion of these goals.

The last part of your goal statement will be in the fifteen years-plus time frame. Typically, this time frame is long-term enough that saving a small amount each month is enough to reach the goal, thanks to compounding interest. For example, if you are forty years old today and save $500 at the end of every month for twenty-five years, with no interest, you will have saved $150,000 dollars. However, if your investment compounds monthly at an annual rate of 6.5 percent, your $150,000 will grow to almost $375,000. That means you turned $500 per month into almost $375,000 simply by deciding to prioritize your future above your daily Starbucks latte, weekly dining out adventure, and the monthly gym membership you never use.

When you shorten the time frame and turn your time horizon of twenty-five years into a time horizon of fifteen years, at the same monthly compounded 6.5 percent annualized return, you must increase the monthly contribution from $500 per month to approximately $1,234 in order to realize that same amount of approximately $375,000. You tell me: which is easier to build into your budget today?

Once you outline your goals and the time frames in which you want to achieve them, you can begin adding details. You can start to assign dates. You can assign specific dollar amounts. You can switch priorities year by year. You can delete goals and replace them with new goals. The point is, you can begin to take control of your future instead of the unpredictable future dictating what will happen to you.

TIP

Filling out a goal statement helps keep the "carrot" in front of you, which in turn helps create motivation. The goal statement also allows you to see what you have accomplished, which helps with validation. Validation encourages additional positive behavior.

The Self-Assessment

If you have been following along and building your balance sheet, budget, and goal statement, then you have a pretty good idea of your financial health. Now you need to start reflecting on how easy, or difficult, this process was to complete. If you found this process to be pretty easy, then I would classify you as a "doer." You are probably comfortable with numbers and understand that managing today's lifestyle in line with tomorrow's goals is an ongoing give-and-take.

On the other hand, if you had a difficult time putting some of these pieces together and you would probably prefer to have someone else handle the process for you, then I would consider you a "delegator." You are probably the kind of person who is either busy with other daily responsibilities and needs to have someone run numbers for you, or you might be a very creative, hands-on, or artistic person, and numbers make you uncomfortable. You prefer to have someone else get into the weeds, do the dirty work, and then give you the overview once they complete the detailed analysis.

Regardless of which type of person you are, the doer or the delegator, you need to determine where your time is best used. In every meeting, I ask clients what their most valuable asset is, both today and when they retire. Usually they cite their house or their retirement plan. While those are probably very valuable, there is something even more valuable: time. Time is the one asset you can never create more of. Every hour you spend doing something that you could have redirected to a more pleasurable or productive activity is an hour lost. In economics this is called the "opportunity cost." The opportunity cost of spending time on mundane tasks rather than with friends, family, hobbies, traveling, and so on is a cost you may never get back.

We will dive into the concepts of being a doer or a delegator in the next chapter. For now, just know your time is valuable, and if performing the tasks outlined in this chapter has tested the limits of your attention span, you might be the type of person who prefers bringing in a team to support you rather than taking on the responsibility of daily management.

To ascertain what you are good at and what you need help with—to develop self-awareness, in other words—is one of the hardest tasks in a person's life. Self-awareness often comes from an epiphany moment where you clearly understand a personality trait about yourself that you previously had not—the quintessential cartoon light-bulb moment when suddenly everything is clearer than it had been before. When you are able to grasp certain truths about yourself, like the fact that you are only human and your days on this earth are numbered, then you begin to prioritize activities in your life around maximizing the moments you have left. You are a smart person and can do so much. But if you are spending your time doing tasks that take away from other, more enjoyable, or important activities, then are you really maximizing your time?

As you perform a task, I encourage you to ask yourself these questions: Is this something I enjoy? If not, is it something I can hand off to someone else? If you can hand it off to someone else, is the expense of having someone else complete that task worth the hour(s) you regain in your daily living? I will let you be the judge of that. Think carefully. This question is of vital importance to making the master plan discussed in the following chapters work for you.

CHAPTER 4

Just Do It ... or Delegate It!

It is amazing what human beings are capable of when we are put into trying situations. You hear of people performing amazing feats of bravery in the face of life-threatening danger. Or the kind of everyday heroism of people who proudly and tirelessly serve their community, like firefighters, police officers, and teachers. Yet to perform at your peak all the time, every day, and in all areas of life would be a tall order. You can end up being a "jack of all trades but a master of none" if you constantly try to solitarily take on every challenge that comes your way.

Becoming the best at everything you attempt would require an endless amount of time and devotion, leaving little time for other life experiences. This chapter addresses the dilemma of trying to handle everything on your own versus focusing on what you excel at and tasking someone else with the rest—being a doer versus being a delegator.

To Do or Not to Do

When I was thirty-two years old, I wanted to go back to school to get my MBA, so I applied to a full-time, fifteen-month Executive

MBA program. Six weeks after I had enrolled, my wife asked me for a divorce and my job took a turn for the worse. Faced with this unexpected crisis, I could have suspended the MBA while I dealt with the divorce on an emotional level and focused on the kids. Instead, I realized my only limits were mental barriers I imposed on myself. So I rose to the occasion, put myself through the Executive MBA program, excelled in my job, spent as much time with the kids as I could, and picked up the pieces of my emotional life.

That trying experience opened my eyes to what I was capable of, which was integral in teaching me how to efficiently run multiple companies, write this book, host multiple podcasts, and spend time with my kids and family. But I also counted on others to support me when I needed a helping hand. Today, if were not for certain people in my life, I am not sure I would be able to keep going at the pace I do. The bottom line is that I learned that I am both a doer and a delegator, depending on the challenge at hand. I do what I am capable of and delegate the rest to those I trust and who I know will do a great job.

Doers

So what does it mean to be a doer when it pertains to your finances? Doers take charge, like to learn new skills, and prefer managing things themselves. However, as I frequently explain to clients, while it is vital to take an active role in assessing and managing your financial situation, it is equally important to know your limitations. Managing a weekly budget, saving into the correct accounts to maximize growth and minimize taxes, and figuring out where to invest your money may be the extent of your abilities. Figuring out how to reduce your annual tax bill or how to withdraw money from your investments when you have retired may not be something you care to learn about.

Knowing your limitations is extremely important to making sure you are not overextending yourself or missing out on life's opportunities because you decided to tackle a new challenge instead of delegating that task to someone else.

There is a lot that can be said about doers. Often, they are Type A personalities. They usually like to maintain a level of control over a situation and know what is going on at different times. Some doers like to make a game out of different tasks and compete against themselves. At times, I challenge myself to complete a task according to a set speed or efficiency benchmark in order to keep it engaging.

The do versus delegate dynamic is different when there are other people in the equation besides you, such as a spouse. The doers I regularly engage with in private practice lead the charge on many aspects of their life. If they are married, they may be more dominant in certain areas of the marriage, while their spouse oversees other areas. When one spouse takes a much more active role in the daily management of the bills or investments, the other spouse may feel secure about letting go of that responsibility. Years might pass in this fashion: one spouse remains entrenched in the day-to-day finances while the other stays focused on other aspects of the household. However, while this approach may work for a long time, there eventually comes a pivotal moment where this division of labor breaks down and can lead to complete confusion, or even chaos. That moment is death.

You are probably thinking, "Well, we don't have to worry about that because I am not planning on dying anytime soon." I hope you are right! The sad truth though is that we do not know when our day of reckoning will come, and if we have not prepared our spouse for that tragedy, how much help are we really providing them? In that situation, the bereaved spouse is suddenly forced to decipher the balance sheet and monthly budget, figure out what the investment strategy should be for future goals, and puzzle over how to minimize their tax burden now that their taxes are going up since they've lost their "Married, Filing Jointly" classification.

I'm not asserting that your loved one would be unable to carry on the torch in the event of a catastrophe, but I am cautioning you to consider how prepared they are to take over where you the doer left off. In the cases of the many widow(er)s I have worked with, the learning curve to understand investments, taxes, and estate planning can be quite steep. Often, it requires weekly or biweekly meetings for six months to a year just to teach them the basics of finances. While I enjoy spending that time with them and helping them through this difficult period, I can only wonder if they would have been better prepared if the doer they were married to took the time to share their approach and process.

In the time I have spent working with thousands of individuals and couples, I have witnessed innumerable, life-changing aha moments. One such moment is when clients honestly self-assess what they and their spouse are—and are not—capable of doing. Too often, people seem to believe that delegating remedial, or sensitive, tasks is not appropriate and that it's better if they do them on their own. This is when I try to point out what it means to be a delegator.

TIP

Next time you are planning to fix the plumbing, repair the garage door, or rake the leaves outside, I want you to think about the time it will take to complete the task, how much energy will be expended, and the frustration that will arise from the project. Then assign a value to the project and ask yourself if taking on the project is worth the time spent, the energy expended, or the frustration experienced. If you determine that it would be better to have someone else do it, then you need to go back to your balance sheet or budget and figure out what goals need to be reprioritized so you can afford to pay someone else to complete the project.

Delegators

Mothers are the some of the most intimidating people on the planet. Watching a frazzled mother with three kids deftly manage the house can be amazing. When I was married, I was in awe of what my then-wife could accomplish in a single day. A typical day might look like this:

1. She got up at 6:00 a.m. to get the kids ready.
2. She made breakfast before school (usually when our child was under the age of six).
3. She got herself ready for the day in record time before heading out to school.
4. She dropped the kids off at two separate schools, since my kids are eight years apart in age.
5. She worked an eight- to nine-hour day before picking the kid(s) up at an after-school friend's house.
6. She got home by 5:00 p.m. to start dinner and work on homework with the kids.
7. She had dinner ready by 6:00 p.m. and I would be home between 6:00 p.m. and 6:30 p.m.

8. She had a little bit of down time before it was time to get ready for bath time or bed.
9. She would begin packing lunches and doing laundry by 8:30 p.m.
10. Finally, she would crawl into bed by 9:30 p.m. or 10:00 p.m. and begin to unwind before falling asleep at 10:15 p.m.— assuming there wasn't a crying child calling out for Mommy.

Now before I start getting hate mail from anyone who demands to know, "What the hell was he doing while she was being Supermom?" let me say that I did help. Unfortunately, I had to spend an hour (each way) in bumper-to-bumper traffic to drive the twenty miles to and from work. I was usually out the door shortly after the kids got dressed in the morning and usually home in time for dinner twelve hours later. Whenever I could, I would share in some of the morning and nightly activities like dressing, bathing, and reading books. But it was Mom who really held things together.

My ex-wife is an amazing mom and takes the concept of being a doer to the max. But how did she find the time to handle all the other demands of daily life? By delegating. The point is that when you are so busy in your daily life, you need to think about what, and to whom, you can "outsource" certain things.

Delegating is so important to one's health and sanity, and I don't just mean in a professional capacity. It improves the quality of your personal and family life too. It wasn't until later in life that I realized the time I had spent working and traveling took away some precious moments with the kids in their younger years. Had I rethought my life's plan and delegated more of my work responsibilities, I might have been able to make it home earlier, which would have allowed me to spend more time with the kids, and my wife. Hindsight can be really frustrating, though I guess it is an unavoidable part of life to make our own mistakes in order to learn and grow on our own.

Early on in my career, I thought I could do everything for everyone. I strove to excel at everything, which would make me the best financial planner to each client I worked with. Then I came to realize that each day was limited by physics and my health. Once I acknowledged I could not bend time and was not invincible, I started to surround myself with people who I knew were experts in their field. These experts became an extension of me and allowed me to help even more people. If you could surround yourself with financial professionals you trusted, how much easier would that make your life? Wouldn't it be great to know that if something went wrong at work or in your personal life, you had a team of people to analyze that problem and come up with a solution instantaneously?

Most of us are constantly on the go. This requires us to assess the tasks we can *and* want to do on our own. For everything else, we need to find the right people to whom we can delegate the rest. In the following chapters, as we delve deeper into the "master plan," choosing whether to do something or to delegate it will be a recurring theme.

CHAPTER 5

Sketching Out the Blueprint: General Financial Planning

It was in mid-October, late in the day. Through my window, I could see the thin autumn light playing on the red leaves. I was on the phone, trying to come to an agreement with my ex-wife on what my youngest daughter's Halloween costume would be, when one of my colleagues suddenly appeared at my door.

"Sorry, Jonathan. There's a gentleman downstairs who says he has an appointment with Chris, but he's not working today, and no one else can take him. Any way you can talk to him?"

I had been planning to leave a little early to pick up my daughter's costume, but something told me to give this mystery client a chance.

When he walked into my office, I could see he had been crying, but he carried himself with dignity and poise—the quiet grace of someone in mourning. I introduced myself, and he smiled. Then I walked him back to one of our conference rooms—and so began a meeting with an individual who would soon become one of my best clients.

He started by saying he did not really know why he was there. He had talked on the phone with someone in one of our call centers who had convinced him to come in based on some recent events in his life.

I told him, "Well, let me see what we can do and if I can be of any assistance. . . . What is the one thing you want to walk away from this meeting having answered?"

Before he could answer, his eyes became puffy as tears gathered in his eyes. "I'm sorry," he murmured, "I just lost my wife and I have a lot of questions."

I reached over for the box of tissues, handed them to him, and said, "Let's see what I can do to help. Tell me about your wife."

We talked for a long time, and I'll tell you more about what we discussed later in this chapter—but first I want to provide some background on the concepts we discussed.

Beyond the Self-Assessment: Some Numbers to Keep in Mind

In chapter 3, we discussed the importance of performing a self-assessment, which consists of three parts: building a monthly cash flow statement (i.e., budget), constructing a balance sheet, and mapping out a goal statement based on short, intermediate, and long-term goals. Performing a self-assessment is not easy. I liken it to standing naked in front of a full-length mirror. Sometimes, your ideal is staring back at you. Other times, the self-assessment exposes unpleasant realities.

In either case, you need to get these three tasks right before moving forward. Making excuses, or hiding behind past experiences, only holds you back. However, facing your fears, facing your mistakes, and facing your financial struggles allows you to construct a foundation to build upon. This foundation will eventually become the process and path to finding your financial freedom.

The three documents of your self-assessment will be the backbone of everything you will use to evaluate your financial situation every year. To be able to use these documents to help you grow and better yourself, it is important to keep five key metrics in mind each time you make a financial decision:

1. Emergency fund
2. Free cash flow
3. Savings rate
4. Debt-to-income ratio
5. Personal rate of return

Emergency Fund

Although considered by some to be old-fashioned, the emergency fund allows you to build up a war chest of money for "what-if" scenarios. Typically housed in the liquid accounts like checking, savings, money markets, and certificates of deposit, the emergency fund traditionally earns market interest rates. Unfortunately, since the Great Recession, interest rates have remained low relative to the consumer price and producer price indices. Money held in low, or zero, interest accounts loses purchasing power to inflation over time.

Therefore, many people have been looking to other ways to create an emergency fund, without holding a lot in liquid reserves. Examples of alternatives are credit cards and home equity lines of credit. It is important to note that I do not recommend these alternative strategies to my clients, because debt acquisition becomes a slippery slope if you have not developed a disciplined saving strategy and have a large after-tax investment portfolio. I am a more "time-tested" planner and prefer to rely on the conventional method of structuring a cash stockpile. There is something deeply comforting about knowing you have cash on hand in case credit markets freeze or hell freezes over.

TIP

Laddering your emergency fund across checking, savings, and short-term certificates of deposit can increase the average yield twofold, threefold, or even fivefold over what your checking account might pay. This could lead to, cumulatively, a few hundred dollars of additional interest over a couple of years., depending upon the size of your emergency fund.

Free Cash Flow

Open up your budget and look at the difference between your net (after-tax) monthly income and your total monthly expenses. This difference is your monthly "free cash flow." Maintaining a positive free cash flow is vital to understanding how much you can contribute to your future goals. The higher your free cash flow, the more you can allocate to your higher financial priorities. Throughout your life, your free cash flow will determine events like sending your child to college, purchasing a house, or appropriately saving for your retirement.

Savings Rate

In order to live in the moment but also plan for the future, you need a balance between spending and savings. Your goal statement will outline and prioritize the goals you need to save for just as your budget will outline and prioritize your monthly expenses. In fact, I recommend thinking of savings as a monthly expense. This way, you can include it in your prioritized list of expenses.

To calculate the required amount of savings from current cash flow that will need to be directed toward each goal, you will need to break down each goal, as in the following examples:

1. Vacation goal ($2,500): $2,500 / # of months to goal (12) = $208.33 per month
2. Car purchase ($25,000): $25,000 / # of months to goal (60) = $416.67 per month
3. College ($50,000): $50,000 / # of months to goal (120) = $416.67 per month

These simple examples illustrate that a family could save $1,041.67 per month ($12,500 annually) to mathematically achieve each of the goals without any portfolio growth or interest. Of course there are other factors that can derail your plan as well. However, as you include various growth rates for the money saved, the amount required to be saved declines—compound interest takes on some of the heavy lifting.

Consider the following average annualized growth rates (compounded monthly) of 1 percent for the vacation fund, 5 percent for the car, and 7 percent for college. By factoring these growth rates into the calculation, your need to save $1,041.67 each month declines to $207.38 + $367.61 + $288.88 = $863.87 ($10,366 annually). The difference between $1,041.67 and $863.87 is $177.80, which can be invested towards, say, retirement, which over a thirty-year time period at an average annualized growth rate of 7 percent (compounded monthly) should yield a future value of $216,910.84. Let that sink in. In this example, you paid cash for one vacation every year until you stop taking vacations, a car every five years, a college education in ten years, and you turned $177.80 per month into $216,910 at retirement in thirty years.

However, to know if you could even save $1,041.67 per month, you need to have a complete grasp on what you prioritize in your budget. The average middle class gross income ranges between $42,000 and $125,000 depending on the state you live in.[1] If we use the midpoint of $83,500, then $1,041.67 per month represents an approximate savings rate of 15 percent. If we adjust your monthly cash flow for compound interest, as noted above, then the savings rate decreases to approximately 12.5 percent ($10,366 / $83,500). This means your required savings rate declines with proper planning, which in turn frees up more of your money monthly to be used on daily living expenses.

While the aforementioned example does not account for building an emergency fund or for other mid-to long-term goals, it illustrates that prioritizing savings as a monthly "expense" allows you to live in the moment *and* save for the future. If you are the kind of family who holds on to cars longer, who takes vacation every few years, or who has multiple children who need to go to college, you can adjust the numbers mentioned above to your personal situation. Remember, while the required monthly savings numbers may seem large today, if you don't start saving they will only get larger as you get closer to your desired "realization date" for each goal.

---

1 Richard Fry and Rakesh Kochhar, "Are You in the American Middle Class? Find Out with Our Income Calculator," *Pew Research Center,* May 11, 2016, http://www. pewresearch.org/fact-tank/2016/05/11/are-you-in-the-american-middle-class/

> ## TIP
>
> At the end of December 2017 the average savings rate in the United States fell to 2.4 percent.[2] This is a perfect example of why completing a balance sheet, a budget, and a goal statement can help you increase your savings rate. If the average American family better prioritized current and future expenses then they could directly control—and increase—their savings rate.

Debt-to-Income Ratio

At some point in every person's life, debt rears its ugly head. Some people are better at avoiding this than others. In college I had a friend who was prone to credit card impulse buys: fancy car accessories, expensive musical instruments he never played, vintage arcade machines. He paid dearly for it in the long run. Although he did get pretty good at Donkey Kong.

The most common form of debt is usually credit card debt, though as we age we add on debt through purchases like cars and homes. However, in order to make larger purchases, we need to qualify for them. Income, debt, and expenses are the three components used to assess the qualification of larger purchases. For example, when purchasing a home, you need to be mindful of your debt-to-income ratio. This ratio is measured by dividing your total monthly debt service (the amount required to make payment on the principal and interest) by your gross monthly income.

---

2 "Personal Saving Rate," Economic Research, Federal Reserve Bank of St. Louis, Accessed February 19, 2018 https://fred.stlouisfed.org/series/PSAVERT

For home buyers, there are two different ratios lenders look at, the front and back ratios.[3] The front ratio includes housing expenses like the mortgage, property taxes, homeowner's insurance, and homeowner's association (HOA) dues. The back ratio includes the same expenses in the front end *plus* vehicle payments, car loan payments, student loan payments, minimum payments on credit card debt, child support, and more. Generally, lenders look for ratios to be less than 28 percent on the front end or less than 36 percent on the back end. Some lenders will accept higher back end ratios but they may increase the interest rate charged to the borrower in order to offset the presumption of higher risk.

Managing your debt, therefore, becomes important in calculating your monthly budget, how much you can save, and whether you will be able to fund your goals. The debt-to-income ratio is an instantaneous way to assess whether you have too much debt. If your debt-to-income ratio is above 35 percent, you need to strongly reevaluate your spending habits as they relate to reaching your future goals. If you service too much debt now, you will not have enough free cash flow to achieve your long-term goals.

TIP

Strictly adhering to the balance sheet, budget, and goal statement will help you manage your debt exposure. This can be important when you carry debt. For example, if you carry $10,000 in credit card debt at a 20 percent interest rate, then in simple interest terms your annual interest would have

---

3 "Mortgage Calculator," https://www.mortgagecalculator.org/calcs/debt-ratio.php.

been $2,000 paid (barring minimum monthly payments made over the prior twelve months). Restructuring your budget and goals can enable you to pay that $10,000 off over a few years which would lead to many thousands saved in interest.

Personal Rate of Return

A "personal rate of return" is the rate of return that *you* need to reach *your* goals.

Even if you don't regularly consume financial news, you probably hear a lot of chatter about the stock market, especially during periods of high volatility. When people are faced with the stock market's meteoric rise or calamitous fall, they use what they hear and see as a personal benchmark for whether their portfolio is doing well or not. But this is a limited perspective.

During the Great Recession, between 2007 and 2009, the US stock market seemed to be in an utter free-fall. This period of high volatility made many investors squeamish and prompted many of them to make ill-planned moves by selling off portions, or even all, of their portfolio. The rationale? "Well if this is *it,* then I am going to keep what little I have left." It was a refrain I heard often during that time, even from experienced investors. It was like a scene from a *Godzilla* movie, if Godzilla was the S&P 500 and the investors were a crowd of fleeing, terrified Japanese. Meanwhile, those of us who had a plan in place and stuck to that plan could sit back and munch on popcorn, knowing it would be okay in the long run.

The reason some people were able to come out of the recession unscathed was because they knew the market would eventually rebound (as it almost always does) *and* because they had built a solid plan around investing for the present *and* for their future. They understood how much portfolio volatility their plan could accept, which portions of their portfolio would experience the most volatility, and most importantly, they had established an emergency fund for events such as the Great Recession. Their investment strategy allowed them to weather the storm because they understood their personal rate of return.

In the world of financial planning, there are two numbers every planner has to contend with. The first is an index's performance at any given moment. The second is the necessary return needed for an investor to realize their desired goal. Everything in life starts with a goal, which becomes the measure by which we determine whether we have achieved a stated objective or are still working towards it. To determine whether the goal is attainable, we must know where our money goes and whether we are spending money on the highest priority things first. Then, when we have free cash flow, we can direct any extra money to the most appropriate accounts on our balance sheet. Filling the right accounts allows the money to compound over an extended period of time, and in some cases to grow tax-deferred.

Once we have our budget under control and are able to direct excess cash flow (savings) to the most appropriate account, then we need to establish an appropriate benchmark for measuring long-term performance. To measure long-term performance, we simply need to understand what growth rate is needed to reach out intended goal(s). This is where things can get technical, but for purposes of this book I will keep it relatively high-level.

Imagine over the next fifteen years you want to take a bunch of vacations, send a child to college, replace the family cars, help support your parents, fix some things around the house, update your wardrobe, and eventually retire. That seems like a lot. Maybe even too much. This is where the self-assessment helps you figure out your current situation. Earlier in this chapter, I pointed out how strategically outlining your goals, the time frame to achieve each goal, and the amount needed to save for each goal showed you how to save. Then I introduced a growth rate associated with each goal to allow for the money you are saving to compound. The compounding effect is what helps reduce the amount of upfront capital needed to achieve your long-term goals.

But how do you know what growth rate to use for each goal? Well, this is the tricky part. There is no one rate for each goal or each time period. Growth rates are influenced by your risk tolerance and your time to reach your goal. In other words, if you want to put a $50,000 down payment down on a home in five years but you cannot save more than $500 per month ($30,000 in five years at 0 percent), then you are going to be forced to accept significantly more risk (market volatility) to make up for any gap in savings. In order to reach the $50,000 goal in five years after saving $500 per month, you would need to average an annualized growth rate of 19.38 percent (compounded monthly), which is a rather high figure. For the sake of comparison, the average annual return of the S&P 500 Index between 1928 and 2016 was around 11 percent.[4]

Needless to say, it would be very difficult to average a 19.38 percent rate of return over any five year period without taking significant risk—*if* it was even possible to find an investment with

---

4 Aswath Damodaran, "Annual Returns on Stock, T. Bonds and T. Bills: 1928–Current," http://pages.stern.nyu.edu/~adamodar/New_Home_Page/datafile/histretSP.html.

that return potential. However, what is important to understand from this example is that the 19.38 percent is *your* personal rate return needed to achieve *your* goal. This growth rate is not based on the stock or bond market. It starts and ends with *your* goal and what *you* could contribute.

What this means, in essence, is that you are in control of your future—even if "being in control" means the freedom to curtail or modify some of your goals. If the rate of return is too high and requires more investment risk or portfolio volatility, then you may be able to accept that your options are fairly simple: lower your goal amount or push out the time to reach your goal. Once you decide what is right for you, then you can build an investment strategy that is directly tied to your portfolio's long-term success *and* satisfies your comfort with risk.

T I P

Make sure your have realistic expectations of what your personal return should be. Too often I hear people say they want to target a 10 percent return, but they are not interested in being 100 percent invested in equities (stocks). To find your personal return for each goal you need to consider how much time is left before your target date for realizing that goal, how much money you can save toward that goal, and how much volatility you can personally accept in all types of market conditions. After this is complete you need to start filling in some numbers in each section and begin to work the plan.

The New Client

Remember the grieving widower introduced earlier in this chapter? During the meeting, we both realized that he and his wife had done an amazing job building a wonderful life together while at the same time saving for their future. We discussed the five fundamental financial areas outlined in this chapter (emergency fund, free cash flow, savings rate, debt-to-income ratio, and personal rate of return), and by the end of the meeting I was able to give him a glimpse into what his financial life would look like as a one-income household.

He was a little in disbelief at how much wealth they had accumulated, but at the same time, his mind began to drift as he started to dream about doing some of the things he and his wife had talked about doing together for many years. He wanted to fulfill the dreams they had discussed together because he believed his wife would be there in memory and spirit to share in these adventures with him. It was a bittersweet moment, but because they had handled their financial affairs well, it had a happy ending. Even now, after all these years in the business, I still marvel at how competent management of five basic numbers can yield such tremendous results.

CHAPTER 6

Protect Yourself: Insurance Planning

"**H**i, Jonathan? . . . It's Barbara. . . . There's . . . there's been an accident."

"Oh my God. . . . I am so sorry to hear that. . . . What happened?"

"Bill had a stroke from a clot in his brain. He was driving on the Beltway and it just hit him. He veered off the road and crashed into the ditch. When the medics arrived they said Bill was conscious, but he couldn't talk or move his right side. The doctors have been running tests since he got to the hospital and believe Bill will recover but they are not sure if he will regain his speech or movement on his right side."

"That is terrible. What can I do to help? Do you want me to call anyone?"

"No . . . the family is on their way to the hospital."

"Do you have his medical POA and living will? Or should I have the attorney fax a copy over to the hospital?"

"No. Our son is going to stop by the house and retrieve them from the safe. . . . Jonathan?"

"Yes, Barbara?"

"Can you remind me what Bill's disability coverage is? I am worried we are not going to have enough money to pay his medical bills and cover our normal bills."

"I will print off a copy of the information I have so we can review it. . . . Would you like me to come to the hospital tomorrow?"

"Yes, . . . I would like that. . . . Thank you. This has all just been too much."

Planning for the Unknown

Planning for the future is never easy. Spending a long time thinking about how your life might turn out can seem like an exercise in futility. But without a clear vision of your future, it becomes too easy to stand still and stagnate, to flutter and flounder. In other words, if you are not driven forward towards something, why do you wake up each and every day? What motivates you or pushes you through the tough times?

Now imagine you know exactly what drives you. Imagine you know the exact reason why you get up every morning at the crack of dawn to fight traffic and sit at a job with a boss you don't really like, then race home for family time, and cap it off with some quality time with your significant other. Whatever drives you to get through your day (and do it all over again tomorrow) is the goal at the end of the long race. The very thing that makes all your effort and sacrifice worth it.

Now imagine everything you have been working toward is taken away from you. Imagine in a blink of an eye, you are no longer able to complete the same tasks that once made up your daily routine. Now, you are completely reliant on others to take care of you, to do the chores you were doing, and to plan your future. Your dreams, your aspirations, your desires are now hanging in the balance—and all because you didn't know how protect yourself and your family.

Enter insurance planning. Insurance planning takes place after you have established your cash flow statement, your balance sheet, and most importantly, your goal statement. These self-assessment documents will highlight your strengths and expose any vulnerabilities in your plan for the future. Then you can work on insurance planning.

There are four areas of insurance planning I strongly encourage clients to review on a periodic basis: property and casualty insurance, disability insurance, life insurance, and long-term care insurance.

Property and Casualty Insurance

In the simplest of terms, property and casualty insurance safeguards your personal property (a home, a boat, jewelry, your prized Big Mouth Billy Bass) in the case of loss, theft, or damage. This kind of insurance is essential, but beware the three most common mistakes people make with their coverage.

Mistake #1: The wrong amount of coverage

Too often, after enrolling in some amount of insurance coverage, we fail to go back and review it. Unless you work with an insurance agent who regularly reviews your policy limits and riders, you could be underinsured or perhaps overinsured. This imbalance usually happens with collectibles, electronics, and jewelry, because people tend to misestimate the value of these things. It is important to take an inventory on your balance sheet at least annually to make sure the items that are most important to you also have the right amount of insurance coverage. Otherwise, the risk of loss, damage, and theft rest solely on your shoulders.

Mistake #2: Not managing deductibles and premiums

Every month, we are faced with paying a service fee for insuring various items in our possession. Sadly, it is all too common to set up the coverage once and just keep paying the bill until the coverage is no longer needed. However, what we should be doing is managing our deductibles and premiums annually. In other words, every year when your insurance company attempts to reprice your insurance coverage, you should call them and either ask for different quotes for the same deductible but a slightly higher insurance amount, or request they keep the insurance amount the same but ask them to quote different deductible amounts, higher and lower than what you currently have.

Completing this exercise should provide you with an opportunity to raise your coverage for little to no cost, increase or potentially keep the same coverage but adjust your deductible, and possibly even reduce your premium cost. This annual review might not lead to any savings initially. However, as your insurance risk declines, as the company reprices the insurance pool within your state, or as your situation changes, you should find some savings from one year to the next.

The advantage of this approach is that it frees up cash flow. Since you've done the self-assessment, you know where your money is going monthly, and if you followed the lessons in the last chapter, you have an emergency fund for unplanned expenses. Therefore, you can consider increasing your annual deductible on your car and house. In other words, by increasing your deductible you are acknowledging that you are going to share in a larger portion of the expense in the event of a catastrophe. The trade-off for increasing your deductible is lower insurance premiums. Performing this task every year can help you find extra savings that could amount to thousands of dollars over your lifetime. Those thousands of dollars should be directed right back toward your goals.

TIP

Based on my observations, reviewing coverage limits, deductibles, and premiums has saved clients $200 to $500 annually. That is $1,000 to $2,500 over five years. Depending on your goal statement, that could pay for a vacation—or two.

Mistake #3: Not having an umbrella for a rainy day

One of the biggest mistakes I see time and time again is not being prepared for unforeseen events. For example, I knew an advisor who worked with a couple whose child went off to college. This student was a hardworking individual who wanted to make a difference in the world. Then one day the advisor received a frantic call from the father that his child had been in an accident. It turned out the young man had gone out to a party one night, driven home, run a stoplight, and crashed into another student's car. Luckily, the other person was not killed, but they did suffer serious injuries.

It wasn't until months later that the parents of the drunk driver received a letter that they were being sued for the accident their child had caused. The parents did not have enough auto coverage limits in place, which meant their auto insurance policy could not completely cover the claims for the other child. In the end, the parents were found responsible for their child's accident and were forced to pay hundreds of thousands of dollars to the other family for damages, future medical bills, and more.

Most of us have insurance for our home and insurance for our car, but what about insurance for life in general? I talk with every new client about their insurance policies, emphasizing that we cannot predict the future and that it is important to make sure they have the right insurance for the right situation.

Unfortunately, your car insurance doesn't protect you from saying something stupid on social media that causes you to be sued for libel. This is where you need an insurance policy that acts as an umbrella, providing coverage for things that do not fit neatly in the world of auto or home policy. Essentially, this umbrella policy provides coverage for events that are not caused by intentional malice, negligence, or willful deceit. In some cases it may cover personal liability issues (like if a visitor trips and injures himself in your home), lawsuits from tenants living in a rental property you own, or even damage to property caused by your pet. Umbrella policies also extend the coverage limits of your auto and homeowner's insurance by "sitting on top" of those other coverages, sort of like how an umbrella protects you from the rain. Because every insurance company has different coverages and requirements, talk to your insurance agent for details. And be sure to read and understand your existing insurance policies to know what your policy will and will not cover.

TIP

In some cases, by spending a few hundred dollars a year to purchase an umbrella policy a household can protect a million of their personal net worth—or more. The most important point is that your insurance coverage not be static. To make sure you have the right coverage in place, with the correct deductibles, evaluate your coverage once a year. Make sure you are not overpaying for insurance you do not need or for coverage you can bear more of the cost for through a higher deductible.

Disability Insurance

Generally viewed by my clients as a "low probability" event, the prospect of becoming disabled later in life is hard for most people to grasp. However, according to the Social Security Administration, in 2017, 2.1 million people filed disabled worker applications.[1] It is probably safe to assume most of those individuals did not believe they would become disabled. Though we often think of disability as resulting from catastrophic, unforeseeable situations like a vehicle accident, this is not usually the case. In fact, in 2012, the top causes for existing disability claims originated from the following:[2]

1. Musculoskeletal/connective tissue disorders (28.9%)

2. Cancer and Neoplasms (14.3%)

3. Injury and poisoning (10.7%)

4. Mental Disorders (9.1%)

5. Cardiovascular/Circulatory (8.7%)

---

1 US Social Security Administration, "Disabled Worker Beneficiary Data," December 2012. https://www.ssa.gov/oact/STATS/dibStat.html

2 Council for Disability Awareness, "Long-Term Disability Claims Review," 2012.

Misconception #1: The definition

According to the Social Security Administration, disability is "the inability to engage in any substantial gainful activity (SGA) by reason of any medically determinable physical or mental impairment(s) which can be expected to result in death or which has lasted or can be expected to last for a continuous period of not less than twelve months."[3]

Over the last fifteen years of helping clients figure out their future, I have realized that people believe they are invincible. This does not mean they think they can run into oncoming traffic and come out the other side unscathed. Instead, it means they presume a lifetime of junk food binges and zero exercise will have no consequences, or that periodically driving while intoxicated is okay. Lifestyle choices that lead to heart disease, stroke, or diabetes are a greater risk factor for disability than freak accidents.

Misconception #2: The types of coverage

So how do you protect yourself from the unknown? Beyond making better life choices, you need to consider where disability insurance fits into your life. Many employers typically offer one, or possibly two, versions of disability insurance. The most common type of employer-sponsored disability coverage is short-term disability, which in my experience typically covers a worker for a period of 7 to 180 days, depending on how much your employer wants to financially support their employees and what they elect as the elimination period (the time that has to elapse before you are allowed to claim coverage, if you qualify). For short-term disability, most employers will continue

3 US Social Security Administration, "Disability Evaluation Under Social Security," https://www.ssa.gov/disability/professionals/bluebook/general-info.htm.

paying between 80 and 100 percent of an employee's base wage. This allows the employee to continue paying their current monthly bills while focusing on recovering in order to return to work.

However, if an employee is not able to completely recover by the end of the short-term disability period, they are required to apply for long-term disability to maintain their benefits and continue to receive income. This is where things can get dicey.

Long-term disability (or LTD) coverage is designed to extend coverage the day after short-term disability lapses. Unfortunately, long-term disability coverage has one major drawback, the coverage amount. Because the average group employee's disability claim lasts 36.2 months[4] and employers continue paying the group's disability premiums while the employee is unable to work, most employer long-term disability plans do not pay more than 60 percent of the employee's income. I have seen some large corporations pay as much as 70 percent of the employee's income, while quite a few others pay as little as 40 percent. This means that during one of the most stressful times in an employee's life, they can expect a large pay cut on top of everything else.

Furthermore, most employers will only provide disability coverage on the employee's base wages, like salary. On rare occasions, employers include variable wages like commissions and bonuses, but in the cases that I have seen, variable wages are only included on a percentage basis.

The bottom line is that you need to be prepared for the possibility that the disability could last more than 180 days, your income will drop, and your expenses will go up as you focus on rehabilitation. To help alleviate the reduction of income and the increase in medical

---

4 Gen Re, "U.S. Group Disability Rate & Risk Management Survey 2012."

expenses, it may make sense to consider acquiring private disability insurance before the potential disability happens. Doing this will not completely solve your problems, but it will help reduce the out-of-pocket expenses by providing an additional ten to twenty percent of pre-disability monthly income benefits.

Coverage is dependent on a number of factors outlined by the insurance company. I advise all clients interested in additional coverage to conduct a separate gap analysis and interview insurance companies about their policies *before* applying. In my experience, if a client is declined by one company and tries to apply with other companies, the other companies tend to be less likely to offer coverage, as they do not want the added risk.

TIP

When applying for private LTD you need to compare the costs and benefits of "Own Occupation" versus "Any Occupation" clauses. The first clause applies to not being able to perform the duties of your own job. The second clause applies to not being able to perform the duties of *any* job. These distinctions are important, because if you are a machine worker and cannot do that job, but you *can* flip burgers at the local fast food restaurant, then an "Any Occupation" would not pay long-term disability benefits.

Misconception #3: Taxes

The last thing anyone thinks about when they are faced with a life-altering change are their taxes. However, they need to keep their tax liability in mind as they reassess their budget. For example, when an employee works, they are subject to ordinary income taxes on the wages they earn. The employee builds a monthly budget around the after-tax income (the income that hits their bank account). But group disability payments are also subject to taxation[5]. Couple this with the reduction of income, and an employee's after-tax income drops even further.

However, with private disability insurance, you are exempt from this tax burden. If you acquired private disability insurance before the incident and then file a claim, the income received is considered tax-free. The rule of thumb to remember when thinking about group disability coverage versus private pay coverage is, "Who pays the majority of the premium?" When the company pays the bulk of the long-term disability premium, they write the premium off against their business income. This means the disability income paid to the employee is subject to an income tax. Alternatively, private disability premiums are paid for by the employee, making the disability income tax-free. Before executing this concept, make sure to verify this information with your insurance agent and tax advisor as laws change.

Understanding the income tax impact of disability income will allow you to better assess the impact on your finances. If you work in a field with a high propensity for incurring a disability, live an unconventional or perhaps risky life, or otherwise have greater health risks, you should strongly think through how a disability can change your life, forever.

---

5 "Life Insurance & Disability Insurance Proceeds 1," FAQs, Internal Revenue Service, Accessed February 19, 2018: https://www.irs.gov/faqs/interest-dividends-other-types-of-income/life-insurance-disability-insurance-proceeds/life-insurance-disability-insurance-proceeds-1

Misconception #4: Social Security Disability Insurance

During my discussion with working clients, I make it a point to review their entire insurance portfolio. I cannot tell you how often I have been told, "If I were to become disabled, I would just apply for Social Security Disability Insurance (SSDI) benefits." Then I ask if they know what it takes to qualify for SSDI benefits—to which they invariably respond that they don't.

At this point I pull up the Social Security website on disability, turn my computer screen toward them, and point out what needs to happen for them to qualify for SSDI benefits *and* how much SSDI could pay in benefits. What follows is disbelief, frustration, and some choice swear words once they learn that in order to qualify, they need to meet the following conditions: "you cannot do work that you did before; we [the SSA] decide that you cannot adjust to other work because of your medical condition(s); *and* your disability has lasted or is expected to last for at least one year or to result in death."[6]

This means that if you are not fully disabled and can work in another field of business, it is possible Social Security may not qualify you for SSDI benefits. Furthermore, *if* you were to qualify for disability benefits, you would never be able to completely replace your pre-disability income, as SSDI is not an income replacement option. Therefore, don't count on SSDI as a fallback option. I always strongly encourage clients to assess their medical situation, their monthly budget, and the field of work they are in, and decide if they can afford to acquire private disability insurance as a way to provide some additional disability protection.

---

6 US Social Security Administration, "Disability Planner: What We Mean by Disability," https://www.ssa.gov/planners/disability/dqualify4.html.

Life Insurance

Today is the day you have always dreaded. It is the day you never wanted to imagine, but here it is staring at you. Today you woke up—the day after your spouse's death—and find your entire world has been turned upside down. The routine you had created together for so many years is now gone. You were the early riser. They took a little longer to make their way downstairs—but when they got down there you had the coffee ready. Both of you went about your individual lives, but when your days ended, you would always meet back at home, share your stories, and spend those twilight hours before bed enjoying each other's company.

Now there is a gaping hole. One that seems too big to fill. Some time passes and daily activities get a little easier, but you are still emotional. Then the day comes where you need to assess your finances and determine how to restructure, retitle, and rebalance your accounts. You quickly realize your expenses have not dropped; in fact, many expenses have even gone up a little since their death. You start to look at your accounts and begin to think about what your financial life will be like with only one income. Your spouse had never been a proponent of life insurance, so they never purchased any more of it than their company offered for free, and now whatever that pays out is not enough to help achieve the goals both of you were saving for.

Now what do you do? Where do you turn? You begin to get frustrated, maybe even scared, about what your future will look like. In fact, you even have the thought, "I wish we had purchased the additional life insurance from . . ."

For nearly a decade I have fought an ongoing internal battle over how much life insurance should fit into my clients' lives. I personally never liked carrying life insurance. I know that might seem odd for a person whose primary responsibility is to look out for his clients' best interest—and who has been to an overwhelming number of client funerals spanning fifteen years. However, for the longest time I thought purchasing life insurance was akin to betting on when I was going to die, and the life insurance was the lottery ticket to my death. I laughed at the notion that I was worth more dead than alive.

Nevertheless, since I started a family, I have come to look at life insurance as a necessary evil, because planning for the future does not just involve me. I realize now that not having an appropriate amount of life insurance would be highly negligent. Therefore, I make it a point to practice what I preach.

With clients, the first step is evaluating the cost for both term life insurance and permanent life insurance in order to minimize monthly costs *and* provide the largest benefit based on the goals outlined in the client's goal statement (chapter 3). Term life insurance is the type of insurance that ends after a specific number of years or when you leave your employer. I liken it to renting (as opposed to owning) an apartment. Once the term ends, your coverage ends, and all of the money you paid into the policy is completely gone.

Surprisingly, more than half my clients tell me they do not carry any life insurance or carry only the group insurance their company offers them. The rest typically carry a separate policy for two or three times what they have in group life insurance, since they want to make sure there is enough to fund more than basic goals like paying the household debt. Other reasons to carry more life insurance might be to replace a portion of the deceased individual's income for a period of time, to fund family weddings, to pay for the children's college, or to fund other goals outlined in the couple's goal statement.

Then there is permanent life insurance, which is akin to owning a home, whereby you make payments (contributions) into the policy. With every contribution, a portion is taken out for the cost of insurance and operating fees while the remaining contribution is either invested or is credited with a fixed rate of return. I explain to clients that over time their permanent policy builds up a cash value, similar to equity in a home, that can later be used to fund other goals or be left alone as an asset on their balance sheet. The goal of permanent life insurance is to remain in force for the entire life of the individual.

These are the two most important questions to answer when it comes to life insurance:

1. If you need life insurance, how much do you need?

2. Do you want to rent your insurance or do you want to own it?

Once you know the answers to these questions, you can begin pricing term and permanent insurance policies. In many cases, I will construct an insurance strategy around a client's cash flow. If the client prefers to "own" more of their policies but wants the most coverage possible, then we look at what they can afford. From there we agree on a target total life insurance amount and begin determining what percentage will be term insurance and what will be permanent. Usually, the term insurance represents 70 to 90 percent of the total coverage amount and the permanent policies make up the difference. As their income increases, we explore the idea of converting some of the term insurance into permanent insurance in order to convert from "renting" more of the insurance to "owning" more of the insurance.

There is no perfect one-size-fits-all rationale for how and why people should carry life insurance. The only question I require clients to answer is, "If you were to die today, what kind of life would you want your family to live in your absence?" That answer opens the door to a much deeper dialogue about their outlook on life, their goals, and what is most important to them. This information is then used to justify or tweak the amount of life insurance acquired.

Long-Term Care

Getting older sucks. Joints crack. Memory slips. Hair falls out. Gravity does horrible things. *The Price Is Right* becomes immensely riveting. But aging is an inescapable fate. What, then, are we doing to prepare for it? The answer I most often hear is . . . nothing. Usually this is not for a lack of understanding that something needs to change, but more because of a tendency to avoid facing the future *and* an uncertainty about what to do. Over the years, I have witnessed so many wonderful people fall victim to the stresses of aging without having a plan. To combat this complacency, I have become relentless about making sure everyone I speak with at least understands their options.

Takeaway #1: You're not alone

Planning for death is probably not on the top of your priority list—though I would venture to say that planning for death might be easier than planning for the final years of your time here on earth, when life comes full circle and you find yourself back in diapers. To think that your children, whom you once bathed, fed, clothed, and cleaned up after, may one day do the same for you is a surreal and probably unpleasant feeling.

In my experience, there are two camps when it comes to the subject of building a senior care plan. One camp says, "I took care of my kids so now it is their turn to take care of me," while the other camp says, "I would rather exhaust every last resource I have before I ever live with my kids and force them to take care of me." It seems that financial resources and personal experience dictate the camp you fall in.

To both sides, I always ask, "If you could create the ideal outcome, what would it look like?" Most people tell me they want financial independence and not to be a burden on those around them. In fact, in a study conducted by the National Institute of Health and National Library of Medicine, 46 percent of people mentioned being a burden as a concern for their later years.[7]

Whether I am talking to my clients or to my own parents, I make sure everyone knows it is essential to have a long-term senior care plan. While "being a burden" is a valid concern, it can be addressed by accepting a level of vulnerability and outlining a senior care plan for the final three to five years of one's life. Doing this allows the elderly individual to have more of a say in the care they receive, and it allows their family to execute on the individual's wishes instead of guessing what that person would have wanted when the time comes.

Takeaway #2: A fear of asking for help

Talking about your finances is rough. It is almost like baring your soul. Next to beliefs on how to raise children or what happens behind closed doors between two consenting adults, financial discussions tend to be held pretty close to the vest. This is one reason why parents usually do not openly talk with their kids about their finances.

Imagine that for forty or fifty years, you have been the patriarch or matriarch of the family and the one to whom other family members

7 Eileen Cahill, Lisa M. Lewis, Frances K. Barg, and Hillary R. Bogner, "You Don't Want to Burden Them: Older Adults' Views on Family Involvement in Care," *Journal of Family Nursing*, August 2009, 15(3): 295–317, https://www.ncbi.nlm.nih.gov/pmc/articles/PMC2825742/.

come for advice and guidance. Then one day you realize they've been coming to you less and less. You realize they look to others for the same advice you once provided. While the shift may have nothing to do with you, it begins to make you wonder.

Years pass and you begin to realize you are not as sharp as you once were or cannot perform the same tasks you once did. It is at this moment you begin to realize you need help from family members you once advised. You may have tried to fight it for some time, but there comes a point where you need to lean on others and reluctantly have to ask for help. This is not to say that you do not welcome another person's point of view. But you have never opened up to another, beyond maybe your spouse, about your finances, and you worry about others telling you how to live your life. Do you let your fears dictate your future, or do you decide to take control and find the help you need? This is when having a trusted advisor, or family member, can help you better assess your financial situation and help you determine if you are properly prepared to finance any future long-term care expenses.

Takeaway #3: The need for long-term care can make or break a financial plan

I cannot stress the following enough: when you are building out your comprehensive financial plan, you *absolutely* need to consider the possibility of needing to pay for long-term care services at some point in the future. The extent of care will depend on you, your family's medical history, where you live, and the type of care you believe you might need. In most planning cases I use today's national long-term care expense averages (roughly, $7,000 per month in a nursing home, or $20 per hour for a home health aide) to gauge funding needs in the future.[8] Doing this will allow you to insert a benchmark for planning purposes that you can adjust as your lifestyle, portfolio, and health change over time.

You must consider two things when it comes to financing long-term care: 1) your assets and those of your family, and 2) government assistance. If you have completed a financial assessment of your retirement and long-term care needs using your cash flow statement, balance sheet, and goal statement and expect that your financial resources will last beyond your projected life expectancy, then you might be able to self-insure. However, for most, the ability to live the lifestyle you want during your retirement years and fund all of your long-term care expenses will typically exhaust every last penny you have. In this situation, it becomes increasingly important to look for an alternate way to reduce the financial drain on your portfolio. This is where long-term care insurance can offer some relief.

There are three widely used long-term care concepts: traditional long-term care insurance, asset-linked long-term care insurance, and life insurance–linked long-term care insurance. Although you should understand the latter two types, this book will focus on traditional long-term care, as it has been around longer and is more widely understood.

When considering traditional long-term care insurance, there are six crucial elements I encourage everyone to review:

1. The ratings of the company
2. Indemnity versus reimbursement
3. Daily versus monthly income benefits
4. No inflation versus adding an inflation rider

---

8 US Dept. of Health and Human Services, "Costs of Care," LongTermCare.gov, 2016, https://longtermcare.acl.gov/costs-how-to-pay/costs-of-care.html.

5. The payout period

6. Coverage limitations

First, the ratings of the insurance company are vitally important, both when you purchase the insurance and every year thereafter. These ratings are made by an independent agency and provide a snapshot of a firm's financial health. While insurance companies have historically had strong ratings due to their residual cash flows from premiums, they are susceptible to many external factors—namely claims. Not being able to meet their claims obligations draws into question their solvency, which means they may not be around when you need them the most. Take as a cautionary tale the case of American International Group (AIG), the insurance behemoth that nearly went belly-up in the Great Recession. Although external factors (rather than problems in the insurance division) were what caused AIG's solvency issues, the point is that you can't always guarantee large firms will be around forever. It is possible for any insurance company to fall victim to larger economic conditions.

Second, before purchasing any long-term care policy, it is important to understand whether the policy will pay claims based on an indemnity clause or on a reimbursement clause. Essentially, an indemnity clause states an insurance company is required to pay you your daily or monthly benefit once you are deemed to be in need of long-term care services, even if your long-term care expenses are lower than your long-term care benefits. In other words, if you have $1,000 in long-term care expenses but are entitled to $2,000 per month, then they are required to pay you the $2,000. This is nice because you can use the other funds to support expenses that are not necessarily covered by long-term care insurance. However, the downside for this optional rider is that you will pay extra in your monthly premiums.

In contrast to indemnity, reimbursement policies require you to submit your receipts to the insurance company first, and they decide which receipts they will reimburse you for. The advantage is that your premiums will be lower, but the biggest drawback is that you will need to have the available funds to pay the expense first before the company reimburses you.

Next, as you build out a quote for a traditional long-term care policy, you will be asked two important questions. The first will be whether you want to quote a daily or a monthly benefit. The second will be whether you want an inflation protection option. My recommendation has always been to request a quote for a monthly benefit with an inflation rider of at least 3 percent. If you elect the daily benefit and your claims are evenly distributed on a daily basis, there may be times where your expenses exceed your daily insurance benefit, which means you come out of pocket on the difference. Additionally, if you do not elect an inflation rider, your insurance benefit will eventually decline via the erosion of its purchasing power over time.

The only alternate option I can think of in lieu of an inflation rider is to have the insurance company quote a higher monthly benefit in an attempt to lock in more favorable rates today and let the purchasing power decline over time. For example, suppose the monthly benefit you were asking for a company to quote was $3,000 per month with a 3 percent inflation rider. That would mean that the $3,000 benefit would inflate to approximately $6,280 in twenty-five years (assuming an annual compound). Therefore, if you requested the insurance company provide you with a quote today for, say, $6,300 per month and no inflation rider, you would maintain a higher benefit in the earlier years, the breakeven for the two scenarios would be around twenty-five years, and after twenty-five years you would see the purchasing power of your monthly benefit begin to diminish, since the $6,300 is not growing beyond the original twenty-five year calculation.

The fifth concern, the payout period, is probably one of the most difficult aspects to make a decision about, since it basically asks you to predict the future and guess for how long, if ever, you will need long-term care insurance. The average nursing home stay is approximately two years, according to the American Association of Long-term Care Insurance.[9] But if you factor in all forms of care, like adult daycare, assisted living care, nursing home care, and potentially memory care, you could be looking at much longer than two years. Therefore, you need to ask yourself what your probability for care will be and how long you want to plan for. I generally suggest clients consider four to five years of coverage if they believe they will use more than just nursing home care.

Coverage limitations are merely an understanding of what the policy will pay for. Examples include, but are not limited to the following:

1. Daily care expenses
2. Who can qualify as a caretaker if you receive care at home
3. Whether your policy can be used in a different country
4. Whether your policy is an indemnity or a reimbursement policy

Knowing the limits before you need care can help you budget better.

---

9 Jesse Slome, "What Is the Probability You'll Need Long-Term Care? Is Long-Term Care Insurance a Smart Financial Move?" American Association for Long-Term Care Insurance, http://www.aaltci.org/long-term-care-insurance/learning-center/probability-long-term-care.php.

Takeaway #4: If you do not build it, it will be done for you

If you take nothing else away from this chapter, please remember this fact: if you do not build your plan, someone else will, and they will most likely not have your input if you are incapacitated or are unable to provide timely input. Too many times I have seen grown children forced to decide the type of care their parents will be placed in, and in many cases the children end up second-guessing their decision. If the facility or the type of care received is not a good fit, the stress of "placing mom or dad in a home" can wear on the family. If you do nothing else outlined in this book, please sit down with friends or family and explain to them your desires about senior care planning. The last thing you want is for your wishes not to be carried out or for your family to be burdened with making life decisions on your behalf.

In the Blink of an Eye

Remember Barbara, whose husband had an accident on the Beltway? When tragedy struck, we already had a well-rounded financial plan that addressed all of the areas discussed in this chapter. Nevertheless, a comprehensive plan without action is nothing more than a binder on a shelf collecting dust. Bill did have disability coverage through work and a private policy to supplement it, but he and Barbara had turned down long-term care insurance due to their family's medical history—his family had a higher-than-usual occurrence of premature death. Barbara and Bill had felt their savings would be sufficient to fund their retirement even if a need for partial long-term care arose. Unfortunately, becoming disabled many years before retirement meant he was not able to maintain the family's savings rate, their expenses increased, and they had to dip into their retirement funds much sooner than they had expected.

While financial professionals can build elaborate and well-conceived plans, the ultimate decision on how to proceed rests solely in the hands of the clients. Therefore, I strongly encourage all clients to consistently revisit their financial plans with advisors at least annually to address any changes. Ask questions. Delegate responsibilities if necessary. And always, always be prepared. Life can change in the blink of an eye. But with the proper planning, those changes won't overwhelm you.

CHAPTER 7

A Tale of Risk and Reward: Investment Planning

The most fascinating investing experience I have witnessed to date had to do with an investor who turned a $500,000 investment into nearly $4,000,000 in the span of seven weeks.

That day started out like almost any other day. It was mid-August, and I had just returned from a trip to Atlantic City. I was feeling pretty good about myself considering I paid for the entire weekend trip with my winnings from the craps table. I am not an avid gambler but I do enjoy a good adventure from time to time.

That afternoon, I was going through a list of people I had to call to introduce myself. New prospective clients, mostly high-net-worth people, the usual suspects—people who had earned their money rather unglamorously, making smart but conventional investments that gradually grew over the course of many years.

But one person on that list stood out. I'll refer to this person with the non-gendered pronoun *they* for sake of anonymity. They were self-made, had worked for a number of years in corporate finance, and were pretty intelligent about quite a few topics, as I learned during our phone discussion. They were ambitious, but they were also a stay-at-home parent who focused on their family time first.

As I continued to probe into their goals, investment strategy, and other financial concerns, I learned they had recently invested quite a bit of money in one stock—in fact, almost 70 percent of their entire liquid net worth. Curious, I asked what had led them to make such a risky bet. The investor explained to me that they knew some of the board members, understood the company's business model, and believed heavily in this company's potential.

A red flag flashed in my mind: This had all the signs of insider trading. However, the investor had come to acquire their shares over the course of the last ten months and at varying price points, which didn't fit the pattern of insider trading.

During the conversation, I asked the investor what their goal for this investment was and if they had an exit strategy for the investment. Nearly three-quarters of their net worth was pinned on the success of this young, unproven company. If it tanked (as so many such stocks do), the investor would be ruined.

"Yes," they said, "when it hits $15 per share, I will sell it." At that time the stock was trading around $3 per share and their purchase prices ranged from $2 to $2.50 per share. Of course, I was a little skeptical of this ambitious goal but the investor reiterated their conviction about the company and said it was a golden opportunity, the kind that only comes around once or twice in a lifetime, if ever.

I soon realized there was no way to help them understand the gamble they were undertaking. It didn't matter how much I talked about reducing their concentrated risk or that they might consider diversifying into other asset classes. They were set on seeing this investment strategy to the end.

I proceeded to have two more calls with the investor about other topics pertaining to broadening their tax and estate plans. Meanwhile, I watched that stock rise, and within seven weeks of my initial call, it hit the target price of $15. In my last call with the investor I asked what their plan was and whether they were going to sell everything or dollar-cost average out of the position. What happened next shocked me and taught me a lesson that has stayed with me to this day. But before I tell you how this story ended, let's look at the question of risk and how to manage it.

How to Manage Risk

Investment is a process of balancing risk with reward. But portfolio risk can never be eliminated, only managed. Even a US Treasury (bill, note, or bond) that is often used as a proxy for a "risk-free rate of return" is vulnerable to interest rate fluctuation and price volatility.

What, then, should you do to manage volatility within your portfolio? There is no single easy answer, but there are two fundamental principles that can aid you when constructing a portfolio: asset allocation and diversification. Asset allocation is the process by which someone invests in assets with different characteristics, like market cap or investment strategy. Diversification means not investing too much in one asset class, but instead, spreading the perceived investment risk across enough investments to appropriately manage portfolio volatility without sacrificing too much portfolio return.

Harry Markowitz revolutionized investment strategy when he developed modern portfolio theory (MPT) in 1952. One of the central tenets of MPT is diversification through non-correlated asset classes.

Essentially, MPT states that there is an efficient way to manage risk and return using different asset classes. To do this, an investor would assess the risk-adjusted return of every asset class and construct a portfolio of non-correlated asset classes that try to keep the risk within the investor's stated objective for risk tolerance. This may sound easy, but it's not.

In the decades since, other mathematicians and economists have advanced Markowitz's research, but for the average investor, putting this research into practice would mean falling into a morass of complicated formulas and theories that would defeat the purpose of doing it yourself.

Therefore, for most investors, simplicity tends to be the preferred method for building and maintaining any investment strategy. However, in order to build out a simple, cohesive strategy, every investor needs to understand the relationship between risk and return.

The Risk-Return Trade-Off

To explain the relationship between risk and return, we first need to break down the components. Risk can be defined as the chance that an investment will lose value. This means that there are varying degrees of risk for different types of investments. For example, a US Treasury bond will have a very different risk profile from a blue-chip, large-cap stock in the S&P 500. By appropriately determining how much you are willing to lose over a defined period of time, you can select investments that align with your desired risk profile.

Unsurprisingly, return is directly linked to the risk level someone takes. It would be fair to say that the more risk an investor takes, the greater the potential for a higher return over a defined period of time. According to the risk-return trade-off, invested money can potentially deliver higher profits only if the investor is willing to accept a higher possibility of loss. Furthermore, since different types of investments offer different types of risk (i.e., default risk, interest rate risk, equity risk, political risk), it is important to make sure the desired return can be achieved within the specified period of time. Otherwise, the risk level taken for a potential return may not be appropriate for the period of time allotted to reach the original goal. This leads us to the all-important question: How much risk should an investor take for a desired level of return?

Many years ago a company came out with a marketing campaign that was designed to ask the average investor, "What's your number?" The intention was to have the audience think about how much money they needed in order to retire comfortably. While the ad was catchy and thought provoking, it only scratched the surface of a more fundamental question: What does someone need to do in order to achieve a goal?

After reflecting on the underlying principles behind the ad campaign, I reconsidered my outlook on investing. I began to think about what the required rate of return would be to give an investor the best possible chance of reaching their future goal. If an investor could obtain their desired return and corresponding goal with a lower level of risk, then what advantage would there be to chasing market performance? Translation: if an investor's personal rate of return (discussed in chapter 5) is directly linked to their goals, then overall market performance should hold less weight when judging an investor's long-term success.

It is important to note that in order to appropriately measure a person's personal risk and return profile, they need to start with an outline of their short-term, intermediate, and long-term goals, as discussed in chapter 3. Then they need to lay out the appropriate time frames for those goals and determine which resources (i.e., assets or cash flow) will be used to fund a particular goal. This may mean that each goal requires a different rate of return. The aggregate weighted return across all goals should be viewed as the needed "personal rate of return" when measuring the impact of progress toward a financial plan. In other words, the aggregate average required rate of return outlined in a financial plan acts as the investor's personal rate of return. It is then left up to the investor, or their advisor, to determine which accounts should be invested with potentially different risk levels that align with the investor's stated individual goal(s) and overall financial plan.

An investor can attempt to optimize their portfolio's expected return by managing the different risks that impact their portfolio. When done correctly, an investor or their advisor can construct a risk-return trade-off matrix. Unfortunately, this matrix is not static and should be assessed frequently, as different risks can change based on external factors. Therefore, to appropriately optimize the risk-return trade-off taken within a portfolio, a level of active management is required by the investor, or by their advisor. The argument between an active versus passive investment strategy has become a widely debated topic, which we will delve into later in this chapter.

Eye's glazed over yet?? Hang on a little more…

Risk Tolerance Questionnaires

Anyone who has ever worked with a financial professional has probably completed some version of a risk tolerance questionnaire, but these tend to be ambiguous. Half of the time, the questions seem arbitrary. The other half of the time, the answers they produce just seem to raise more questions.

For example, if asked, "How much would the market have to decline before you would sell?" the average investor's answer might be "it depends." While the question is trying to gauge how much volatility or risk an investor will accept, it lacks a qualifier, such as a specified time frame. An investor's answer will probably change as the hypothetical time period increases. While questions like these have the best of intentions, they are difficult to interpret and should be conducted with a qualified investment professional, in order to address follow-up questions that will inevitably arise. It may even be necessary to conduct a risk tolerance questionnaire for different investment objectives or goals. This way, an investor's concerns can be tailored and addressed with the respective resources in mind for that particular goal.

Once the questionnaire is complete, an algorithm attempts to accurately define an investor's risk aversion and correspondingly suggests an asset allocation that matches their volatility preferences. It is my belief that the results of these "general questionnaires" are rooted in math and sample size testing, and therefore "your" risk profile is not so much customized for your needs, your goals, or your outlook on life but rather by a litmus test designed by a company's legal, compliance, and investment department.

My issue is not necessarily with the algorithm, but with the end result. For over a decade I have helped thousands of clients complete some version of a risk tolerance questionnaire. In each instance, the end result was to tell the client they were defined by a risk-tolerance label such as "moderate conservative," "moderate," or even "moderate aggressive." The goal of assigning a risk profile in this fashion is not completely clear to me, and in fact seems rather arbitrary. If I were to guess, it would seem that this standardized risk profiling is designed to help investors understand their risk preference in an easily digestible way. It's also because the big box firms' protocol usually involves checking off a few boxes for CYA reasons. Hopefully in the future, the industry will come up with a better process to determine investors' level of comfort with risk.

One problem with pigeonholing a person with a risk tolerance label is that it might not be an accurate representation of their true comfort level. If an advisor tallies up the results and asks an investor if that particular risk tolerance label "fits" them, the investor is likely to shrug their shoulders and agree. I liken it to a psychologist asking a patient to analyze the patient's own Rorschach test results. Since the Rorschach test and risk tolerance questionnaires are both open to interpretation, the end result might be clouded by someone's personal view or their current mood, or it might be an incomplete assessment. In any case, each individual needs to fully understand the result before accepting it—but also to take the results with a grain of salt.

TIP

When evaluating risk, consider the time frame to achieve a goal and the resources you have to dedicate to the goal. Depending on your comprehensive plan, it may even benefit you to gradually allocate more of your risk to intermediate and long-term goals. In some instances you may have to push your acceptance of risk slightly outside your comfort zone if your time frame is greater than fifteen years. Remember, the more you can remove emotions from your decision making the fewer impulsive decisions you will make. Think of the last impulse hot fudge sundae, or white mocha latte from Starbucks, you made and how much it didn't fit with your workout regimen…emotions at the wrong time can lead to unfortunate circumstances, especially around the waist line.

For Doers: Becoming an Educated, Self-Directed Investor

Becoming an educated, self-directed investor is a worthy goal, but it again comes down to whether you want to "do" or to "delegate." Given the plethora of details and nuances involved in selecting, managing, and rebalancing investments within a portfolio, many investors are not as educated about the entire investment process as they should be. If you choose to go that route, this section will provide you with some key facts, figures, and tools that you can use as you manage your investments. My intention is to provide you with some of the same tools that I use to evaluate an investment. These tools can be used to help you build a well-rounded, diversified portfolio across multiple asset classes. Combine these tools with research you conduct on your own to invest proficiently and prudently.

First, to create a general principle of risk, we need to assess your comfort with volatility and variability. (Variability is "the extent to which data points in a statistical distribution or data set diverge from the average, or mean, value as well as the extent to which these data points differ from each other. There are four commonly used measures of variability: range, mean, variance and standard deviation.")[1] To do this, let me ask you one question: What would you define as a

1 "Variability," Investopedia.com, https://www.investopedia.com/terms/v/variability.asp?ad=dirN&qo=investopediaSiteSearch&qsrc=0&o=40186.

catastrophic loss? In other words, how much of your investment portfolio would you have to lose in the next six months before you became super-scared and hit the eject button? If you had a $100,000 investment portfolio, would you be okay with a $10,000 decline? How about a $40,000 decline? A $75,000 one?

If you are like many investors I speak with, you are probably saying, "I would just sit tight because I know the market is going to bounce back." These investors are usually those who either have over fifteen years before they reach their goal or have a significant level of guaranteed, recurring income, which buffers them against market volatility. But imagine for a moment retirement was going to happen within the next six months and you did not have a guaranteed income stream: Would your comfort with how much you could lose change?

If so, that means that your comfort with risk changes as your circumstances change. Therefore, as you evaluate your goals annually, you need to assess your comfort with risk and determine how much you can afford to lose over the following six to twelve months before you hit the panic button. This doesn't mean all of your investments should be oriented toward a short-term horizon, but rather that you understand how much volatility your portfolio may experience in the short run. Invest for the appropriate time period, be mindful of the aggregate volatility of the whole portfolio, and accept that your chosen level of risk may mean the possibility of losing it all.

Now that we have addressed your comfort with loss, let's talk about some of the statistics that will help you balance the risk within your portfolio. When it comes to risk, there are two mainstream measures every financial professional can use to evaluate an investment. The first is "beta." The second is "standard deviation." Let me see if I can break these down without your eyes glazing over.

Beta is a measure of risk associated with a singular investment. According to Nasdaq.com, beta is "the measure of an asset's risk in relation to the market (for example, the S&P500) or to an alternative benchmark or factors. Roughly speaking, a security with a beta of 1.5 will move, on average, 1.5 times the market return. . . . According to asset pricing theory, beta represents the type of risk, systematic risk, that cannot be diversified away."[2]

It is possible for an investment portfolio to be made up of multiple investments, each with different betas. Unfortunately an investment's beta is unique to itself because it is based on the characteristics of that particular investment. Since beta is unique, it cannot be measured and compared on its own across different investments. This requires you to also look at another metric when evaluating risk: standard deviation.

The textbook definition of **standard deviation** is "the square root of the variance. A measure of dispersion of a set of data from its mean."[3] That might make no sense to you, but if you think back to high school or college math, you were probably taught about the bell curve. When the bell curve represented a normal probabilistic distribution, you had the mean (average) return sit squarely in the middle of it. The professor would then ask you to calculate the probability of a 68 percent outcome, a 95 percent outcome, and lastly a 99.7 percent outcome. These outcomes were correlated with one deviation, two deviations, or three deviations, respectively, away from the mean

2 "Beta Definition," Nasdaq.com, http://www.nasdaq.com/investing/glossary/b/beta.
3 Sal Khan, "Measures of spread: Range, Variance, and Standard Deviation," Khan Academy, https://www.khanacademy.org/math/probability/data-distributions-a1/summarizing-spread-distributions/v/range-variance-and-standard-deviation-as-measures-of-dispersion.

return on both the positive and negative sides (i.e., on either side of the mean). This is known as the "68–96–99.7 rule" or the "empirical rule" in statistics.

Let's walk through a quick example. Say your portfolio's average return for the last ten years ended up being 7 percent. Assume that over that time you had not made any changes to your portfolio. Now let's say someone told you the portfolio's standard deviation for your portfolio based on the variability of the underlying investments was 10 percent. To calculate the variability of your portfolio, you would add 10 percent to 7 percent to find out the positive side of the bell curve and subtract 10 percent from 7 percent to find out the negative side.

The result would be a positive 17 percent and a negative 3 percent, which would represent a 68 percent probable outcome. This means that during that ten-year period, your portfolio had a 68 percent chance of ending up somewhere between +17 percent and 3 percent. If we continued with the example, then a 95 percent probabilistic range would result in a portfolio range of +27 percent to a negative 13 percent and a 99 percent range would result in a +37 percent to a negative 23 percent range.

Standard deviation measures a portfolio's total risk as opposed to measuring the systematic risk (beta) and other risk factors. To determine whether standard deviation is an appropriate measure to assess a portfolio, there are many other complex calculations you need to consider, but to keep things simple you need to find a portfolio range you are comfortable with.

A few paragraphs back we talked about deciding what a devastating loss could look like. You picked a number that you were comfortable with. If we interpreted that devastating loss in terms of a percentage, you would know what your 99 percent maximum loss would be. If we stick to the example above, on $100,000 with a target return of 6 percent and a standard deviation of 15 percent, then you would be willing to accept a maximum (three standard deviation) swing from +51 percent to a negative 39 percent in your portfolio. This would result in a potential maximum loss of $39,000 over the following six months.

It is important to note that markets are not predictable and the underlying investments are even less predictable, which means it is possible to experience an outlier beyond a 99 percent probability. The takeaway here is to understand that deciding on an acceptable range of portfolio variability will help you better assess your next steps.

After you have decided how much money you are willing to lose and have come up with a projection in terms of percentages, then you can turn your attention to what we call the **correlation coefficient** and **coefficient of determination**. Bear with me again as I try to get through some of the technobabble.

Correlation coefficient tells the story of "how well a linear model describes a relationship between two variables."[4] In other words, how strongly correlated one variable's outcome is to another variable's outcome.

On the other hand, "the coefficient of determination is used to explain how much variability of one factor can be caused by its relationship to another factor. It is relied on heavily in trend analysis and is represented as a value between zero and one. The closer the value is to one, the better the fit, or relationship, between the two factors. The coefficient of determination is the square of the correlation

---

4 Sal Khan, "Example: Correlation Coefficient Intuition," Khan Academy, https://www.khanacademy.org/math/probability/scatterplots-a1/creating-interpreting-scatterplots/v/correlation-coefficient-intuition-examples.

coefficient, also known as 'R,' which allows it to display the degree of linear correlation between two variables."[5]

What does all of that mean? Simply stated, when you are looking at beta, you need to know how closely correlated the results of the investment you are researching are as compared to their corresponding benchmark. If the coefficient of determination is greater than 0.70, there is a good fit relationship between the investment and the corresponding benchmark. If the coefficient of determination is less than 0.70, you are better off analyzing the investment's standard deviation instead of its beta in order to assess the single investment's performance.

Why? Because a coefficient of determination of less than 0.70 means there are additional external factors that the benchmark does not include that are contributing to the investment's performance. When a coefficient of determination is less than 0.70, you should turn your attention to the investment's standard deviation, since standard deviation measures the variability of all risks affecting an investment instead of those just contributing to beta.

Thus far, we have discussed what a devastating loss is for you. We have figured out how much variability you are willing to accept in your portfolio. We outlined the need to look at standard deviation and beta when selecting your investments. Now we turn to three additional tools that can help you assess your portfolio's success. They are Sharpe, Treynor, and Jenson, or alpha.

It is not enough to just evaluate an investment based on its risk characteristics. You may find some investments that have very low risk but also have a very low return. Therefore, you need to understand

---

5 "Coefficient of Determination," Investopedia.com, https://www.investopedia.com/terms/c/coefficient-of-determination.asp.

how to use risk-adjusted return metrics. To do this, you need to look at the following:

Sharpe Ratio
(Expected return of an investment – the risk-free rate) /
Investment's standard deviation

The expected return of an investment is the anticipated return for the coming time period. You can calculate the expected return, but it requires additional time and calculations. For purposes of this illustration, we will not expand on the complexities of calculating expected return.

The risk-free rate is simply an asset that is considered "risk-free." While there are technically no investments in the world that are 100 percent risk free, for most calculations, investors use US Treasury bills, notes, and bonds as proxies (each dependent on the time period being evaluated).

According to Morningstar, "the higher a fund's Sharpe ratio, the better a fund's returns have been relative to the risk it has taken on. Because it uses standard deviation, the Sharpe ratio can be used to compare risk-adjusted returns across all fund categories."[6] Measuring an investment on a risk-adjusted basis helps to better evaluate how it will fit into an investment strategy.

Treynor Ratio
(Expected return of an investment – the risk-free rate) / Invest-
ment's beta

Jordan Wathen of The Motley Fool, a popular investment advice website, states, "Investors and academics have long sought for a way

---

6 "The Sharpe Ratio Defined," Morningstar.com, http://news.morningstar.com/classroom2/course.asp?docId=2932&page=4.

to compare the performance of portfolios on a risk-adjusted basis. If you can adjust for risk, you can directly compare the performance of portfolios that have little or nothing in common, like a corporate bond portfolio to a stock portfolio, for instance. The Treynor ratio does just that. It calculates an investment's performance per unit of risk."[7]

By looking at an investment's risk characteristics on a per unit basis, you can begin to compare one investment to another and determine which individual investment will offer better individual returns. Then as you select the individual securities with varying betas, you can refer back to the coefficient of determination to measure the investment's performance against its comparable benchmark. Finally, as you bring your selected investments together, you will want to run some tests to determine what kind of portfolio standard deviation you can expect. This way you can make sure your portfolio's variability stays within your target range. To do this, you will need to calculate the portfolio's standard deviation.

The last formula you should look at is Jenson, or alpha. This is a measure of excess return above a benchmark. There are ways to determine how much excess return is to be attributed to skill and how much to luck, but unless you want to run a handful of other calculations, let's keep this simple.

As you perform your research, you will be able to calculate, or look up, the investment's historical alpha metrics. All you really need to know is that a positive alpha means the investment management team has outperformed their corresponding benchmark. The higher

---

7 Jordan Wathen, "Use the Treynor Ratio to Measure Your Risk-Adjusted Portfolio Performance," The Motley Fool, June 9, 2015, https://www.fool.com/investing/general/2015/06/09/use-the-treynor-ratio-to-measure-your-portfolio-pe.aspx.

the alpha, the higher the excess return the portfolio's investment team returned to investors. If you can find investments that have historically provided **a positive alpha, a lower beta or standard deviation**, and **a high coefficient of determination**, you are on the right track to building a solid portfolio strategy.

It is important to note that past performance does not guarantee future results. Therefore, you need to conduct additional research into the investment team's background, the investment's track record, the governance history, and any additional facts you feel are important before making an investment decision.

Whew! That was a lot. I hope you didn't toss the book across the room or stick it under a table leg to balance a rickety table. My goal in providing these explanations was to make it clear that being a self-directed investor involves a fair amount of work for building even a simple cohesive investment strategy. Thinking you can just hastily pick some investments, let them run for a few years, and then come back to see how the portfolio has done is the wrong approach. Would you buy a new car and only take it in to the mechanic five years later for your first oil change, your first tire rotation, or your first tune-up? I hope not.

Being a self-directed investor means you need to take an active role in managing your portfolio. Otherwise, your financial plan's trajectory is likely to drift off course as time progresses and things change. If you do not know where you are now, how will you know where you are going?

Asset Management Services: For Delegators

If you decide to delegate the management of your portfolio to others, you need to understand what types of asset management services exist. There are three broad categories of asset management services that investors use to make investment decisions:

1. Periodicals, magazines, and newsletters
2. Robo-advisors
3. Professional money managers (aka investment adviser representatives, or IARs)

The first resource (periodicals, magazines, and newsletters) is widely used by self-directed investors who either enjoy researching investments, like to be actively involved with their portfolio, or believe there isn't one "best source" for information. Unfortunately, this process can be labor-intensive, and if this group of investors begins to lose interest or other goals compete for their time, their investment plan can fall apart.

Additionally, the abundance of tips, projections, and commentary give periodicals and newsletters a certain flashy allure for investors, but the authors of these articles may be dubiously qualified to dispense advice (think back to some of my comments about financial bloggers as another example). Also, authors of these publications may be providing a point of view without the securities licensing a financial advisor or investment adviser is subject to by regulatory bodies such as FINRA and the SEC. Therefore, if you are someone who reads different periodicals or newsletters, make sure the person putting out the content is a qualified investment professional. Also recognize that advice disseminated for a wide audience is not the same as advice specifically tailored to *your* risk profile and financial needs.

Robo-advisors, the second asset management resource, are essentially the marriage of traditional investment management with computer algorithms. Generally, robo-advisors select investments within their investment pool, invest client funds into the selected portfolio, and periodically rebalance an individual's investments.

TIP

The Investment Adviser Act of 1940 states, "publishers are excluded from the Act if advice is provided impersonally, is "bona fide," and is of general and regular circulation."[8] Therefore people talking to a wide audience—for example, on TV, on the radio, or in books (like this one)—are not held to the same standard as advisers, and advisors, who provide one-on-one advice. It is important to note that this book was written for the masses and does not provide individually customized advice. However, I am holding myself to a higher standard, the one I use in private practice, when conveying my thoughts and perspectives to you.

There are two significant distinctions that make robo platforms different from traditional investing. First, many robos subscribe to the market efficiency premise by investing in broad, low-cost indexes through exchange-traded funds (ETFs) instead of in specific market strategists. Second, according to The Motley Fool, "the primary wealth management service that robo-advisors offer is periodic rebalancing."[9]

---

8 "Regulation of Investment Advisers," US Securities and Exchange Commission, Accessed February 19, 2018: https://www.sec.gov/about/offices/oia/oia_investman/rplaze-042012.pdf
9 James Watkins III, "The Unanswered Question About Robo-Advisors," *The Motley Fool*, Feb. 21, 2017, https://www.fool.com/investing/2017/02/21/the-unanswered-question-about-robo-advisors.aspx.

From the ashes of the Great Recession rose multiple robo-advisor platforms. Companies like Wealthfront and Betterment took the idea of algorithm trading to the general public, based on the philosophy that markets are efficient and the average investor will not "beat the market" no matter how well-informed he is or how clever his trading strategies are. There is some truth to this as it is a challenge for anyone, even experts with a finely tuned methodology, to consistently predict the future.

With the central tenets being that "markets are efficient" and, according to MPT, that asset allocation (i.e., the makeup of asset classes that investors invest in) determines over 90 percent of a portfolio's average return, robo-advisors no longer needed to chase portfolio returns and instead could focus on perfecting their process and making it more systematic and efficient. In other words, these companies were able to convince investors that their primary goal was not to beat an index's performance, but rather to create operational efficiencies by rebalancing an investment account periodically based on a customer's goals and market volatility. In return for this service, these firms were able to significantly lower their fees (as compared to financial advisors and IARs), with the average robo-advisor platform charging annually between 0 percent and 0.50 percent for computer-based asset management services.[10]

However, these robo-advisor companies also realized some investors did not want to completely eliminate the human element. To meet this need, they began offering clients the ability to speak with a financial representative, typically one not dedicated to the client, for

---

10 Arielle O'Shea, "Best Robo-Advisors: 2017 Top Picks," Nerdwallet.com, June 23, 2017, Accessed February 19, 2018: https://www.nerdwallet.com/blog/investing/best-robo-advisors/

an additional fee. In some cases, the total advisory fee paid is similar to what the advisors they fired charge today.

Now that you know robo-advisor companies can charge as much as an advisor but for **passive investing**, there is one more thing to consider. If you are a practicing attorney, you may have read through your investment application with a fine-tooth comb. But if you are not versed in legal jargon, you will find, buried in legal disclosures and prospectuses, that these companies have complete discretion over which securities are available on their investment platform. What does this mean?

1. This means that the entire universe of available investments are not necessarily accessible to their clients.

2. Their investment strategies are typically passive, making the need to have additional investments seeking active return, or alpha, less important.

3. After they select an investment for inclusion on their platform, they negotiate a revenue sharing agreement with the fund company.[11] This agreement is their way of being compensated for the lowers fees they charge you.

To conclude my critique of robo-advisors, I will end with this question: *When,* not if, the next market crash unfolds and you are invested in a computer-trading algorithm, who do you hope will talk you off the ledge? Watson? Siri? Alexa?

The third asset management resource, professional money managers or IARs, can be categorized as the "human factor." This is where a professional takes on the role of an investment adviser representative

---

11 Hugh Son, "Your Robo-Advisor May Have a Conflict of Interest," *Bloomberg,* June 27, 2017, https://www.bloomberg.com/news/articles/2017-07-27/your-robo-adviser-may-have-a-conflict-of-interest.

and manages a portfolio of financial securities on behalf of an investor who does not have the time to direct their own investments. The IAR may also look for opportunities to outperform the broad investment markets. Within this category, there are many subsets, but the one many investors are most familiar with is the investment adviser. This person acts as a conduit between the client and an investment research team. Often this person's responsibilities can include but are not limited to the following:

1. Conduct research on markets or securities.
2. Invest funds into financial securities based on research.
3. Actively monitor and rotate investments in and out of a portfolio.
4. Hold investment review meetings with clients.

Where a robo-advisor may take a passive role in portfolio management, many investment advisers subscribe to active management with the goal of outperforming a broad market. One major problem with investment advisers and active investment strategies is the ability to find one with a reasonable investment philosophy and desirable performance track record. For this reason, I encourage investors to learn what their investment firm's unique investment philosophy is, why it was constructed that way, and how it will potentially benefit them if they elect to invest in it.

TIP

An investment adviser who takes a buy-and-hold approach may have a decent investment track record. However they may also just be sitting on your money, collecting fees without

---

providing any concrete active management. As I said earlier, "a broken clock is going to be right twice a day." Make sure you understand their portfolio investment strategy before investing with them. Do not be afraid to ask them questions. If they cannot explain it to you in simplified terms, then either they need to understand how to communicate to their audience better, or you may need to be on heightened alert. While investing can be complicated, your advisor shouldn't being speaking another language to you in review meetings.

Active versus Passive

The debate continues to rage on. Between robo-advisors preaching index investing, Vanguard's founder John Bogle preaching "low cost investing" by avoiding the higher fees of active managers,[12] and the rest of the fund management community touting active management, how is anyone to know the right answer?

According to Mark Hulbert, a columnist at *MarketWatch*, the odds that an active strategy will beat a passive strategy are about one in twenty.[13] He cites Standard & Poor's annually published SPIVA Scorecard,[14] which tracks how active funds have performed over the

---

12 Mitch Tuchman, "Jack Bogle is right: Don't be a passive investor, be a frugal investor," *MarketWatch*, October 7, 2017, https://www.marketwatch.com/story/jack-bogle-is-right-dont-be-a-passive-investor-be-a-frugal-investor-2017-07-25.

13 Mark Hulbert, "This Is How Many Fund Managers Actually Beat Index Funds," *MarketWatch*, May 13, 2017, https://www.marketwatch.com/story/why-way-fewer-actively-managed-funds-beat-the-sp-than-we-thought-2017-04-24.

14 Aye M. Soe and Ryan Poirier, "SPIVA U.S. Scorecard," 2017, http://www.spindices.com/documents/spiva/spiva-us-mid-year-2017.pdf.

preceding one-, three-, five-, ten-, and fifteen-year periods. Digging into the mid-year 2017 scorecard reveals some fascinating facts, like these:

1. Over the five-year period, 82.38 percent of large-cap managers, 87.21 percent of mid-cap managers, and 93.83 percent of small-cap managers lagged their respective benchmarks.

2. Similarly, over the fifteen-year investment horizon, 93.18 percent of large-cap managers, 94.40 percent of mid-cap managers, and 94.43 percent of small-cap managers failed to outperform their respective benchmarks.

3. Funds disappear at a meaningful rate. Over the fifteen-year period, more than 58 percent of domestic equity funds, 55 percent of international equity funds, and approximately 47 percent of all fixed income funds were merged or liquidated. This finding highlights the importance of addressing survivorship bias in mutual fund analysis. Survivorship bias can make a mutual fund company's performance look better than it actually is because underperforming funds are often dropped or merged. Judging performance based only on the "survivors" paints an incomplete picture of things.

The first statistic tells me that nearly 10 to 20 percent of the active managers outperform their corresponding benchmarks over an intermediate period, while the rest underperform. Unfortunately, the number of outperformers declines over a longer time frame, as noted in the second bullet.

I believe there are two reasons why active investment management is perceived as worse than passive indexing. The first is addressed in the third bullet: about 50 percent of the funds that existed over the last fifteen years are no more (due to poor performance, mutual fund company consolidation, investment strategy style changes, or other factors). This means a number of available funds over longer periods of time are no longer used in the calculation. In other words the sample size has shrunk, which makes the number of funds beating their peer group over time less impactful, especially if the successful funds were acquired by less successful and larger funds for a performance boost.

The second reason is the general lack of acceptance among the public that if an investor was actively involved in their portfolio, the way an investment adviser representative or portfolio manager should be, the investor would not necessarily have held the same fund for five years—let alone fifteen years. More simply stated, taking an active role in managing your risk exposure and seeking investments that are positioned to do better from one year to the next can offer an added advantage. An active role in the management of a portfolio allows an investor to increase their opportunity to find securities that meet or exceed peer group returns over shorter periods of time.

The report states that on average, 40 to 50 percent of active managers outperform their comparable benchmark over a one-year period. Therefore, an active investor looking out for opportunity has a much greater chance of outperforming a comparable benchmark with an active strategy than over five, ten, or fifteen years. Now, this does not mean I am a proponent for trading a portfolio (by which I mean, buying and selling based on technical or fundamental markers, and over a relatively shorter duration, like six months to a year).

Instead, as noted earlier in the chapter, taking an active role in the portfolio can offer opportunity to find "diamonds in the rough." You may select one fund that does well and hold it for two years. Or you may acquire one fund today and reduce or eliminate exposure to that fund in eleven months. The point is that you're following the fund's performance more closely and are making trades at a greater frequency than if you were just "buying and holding" for the long term.

Fee No Evil

Another factor you must consider is fees. Where financial professionals add drag to a portfolio is in the fees they charge. If your advisor is charging 1.5 percent to manage your investments, then they'd better be selecting some damn good securities to help offset it. Otherwise, while a gross (before fee) return might meet or exceed a benchmark from one year to the next, the net (after fee) return will drag the portfolio below the benchmark's return.

It's common in the industry to compare performance to a benchmark, but as I stated earlier, you really want to compare your performance to your **personal rate of return**. When your portfolio's net return does not *consistently* meet or beat your financial plan's target personal rate of return, you are jeopardizing your plan's fundamental success.

While we are on the topic of fees, I want to hit on a point that *a lot* of people talk about: the expenses inside a fund (i.e., expense ratios). The conventional wisdom is that in order to keep fees down, you want to find investments that have low, or zero, internal costs. For example, mutual funds and ETFs have internal operating expenses that allow the fund company to operate the fund. Stock trading, on the other hand, does not pass the companies' operating expenses on to the investor; rather, you pay a nominal trading fee to acquire or dispose of the stock.

For simplicity's sake, I will focus on mutual funds in this discussion of expenses. First, I know that many people believe the internal expense ratios should be kept very low in order to keep more money in your pocket. However, investment gurus, pundits, and others fail to point out one simple truth: Nearly all mutual funds report the price per share of a mutual fund as the NAV, or "Net Asset Value." The NAV reflects the net price per share of a mutual fund, accounting also for liabilities and internal operating expenses.

For example, say you have two funds: Fund A with an internal operating expense ratio of 1.0 percent, and Fund B with an internal operating expense ratio of 0.1 percent. Both funds have a NAV on January 1 of $10 per share. Then, on December 31, they both have a NAV of $11 per share. What is their return? Considering the expense ratio has already been deducted from the NAV, and assuming there were zero dividends, then this is how the return for both funds would be reflected:

> January 1 $10
> December 31 $11
> $11 − $10 = $1 gain
> $1 gain / $10 originally invested = 10 percent return

Therefore, both funds produced the same net return despite the difference in fees. So which fund did better at the end of the year? Many investors would say the fund with the lower expense ratio did better because it was able to produce the same return with fewer internal fees. However, if we look at the gross return (by adding the expense ratios back to the net performance), then Fund A's performance was 11 percent (10 percent +1 percent) and Fund B's performance was 10.1 percent (10 percent + .01 percent). Therefore, if Fund A can modify their investment strategy to reduce the internal expenses by more than 0.1 percent, then they will eventually outperform Fund B (assuming everything else remains equal).

This simple illustration is attempting to address the fact that for passive investors who want to take a backseat with their portfolio and let someone else handle the driving, it would be better to choose funds with lower internal costs. But for investors who want to be more involved with the direction of their portfolio and manage its performance to meet their personal rate of return, it would behoove them to evaluate their investment options on a net fee, and net return, basis. This way they can decide which investment option, regardless of the internal fees, would be better suited in their portfolio.

You are probably thinking to yourself, "Uncle! No more information! I'd rather fill out insurance forms, do my taxes, anything else." Though the information in this chapter may be dense, dry, or difficult to digest, it's tremendously beneficial to learn. My goal is to help you expand how you think about your own portfolio and challenge conventional beliefs that you may have heard along the way.

You do not have to agree with me. If all this chapter did was reaffirm the way you view investing, then at least you know the strength of your convictions. If it helped you peek behind the curtain to understand how some portfolio managers, investment advisers, and financial advisors think about investing, now you can use that newfound knowledge to your advantage. And finally, if this chapter made you realize that you prefer to be a delegator rather than a doer when it comes to creating, executing, and monitoring your investment strategy, I have given you some intelligent talking points to fall back on when conversing with your investment adviser.

Tough Lessons

So, what happened with the investor I mentioned earlier—the one chasing those astronomical returns? Once the stock hit $15 a share, I asked the investor what their exit strategy was. To my surprise, they said, "I am going to let it ride and see where it goes." I reminded them that when it was sitting at around $3 per share, they were pretty adamant that $15 was their price target for exiting the position, and I asked why they were now changing their strategy. The investor didn't have a good answer other than to say they wanted to see how much higher it could go. I recommended the investor place some trailing stop loss positions on the stock in order to preserve some of their massive profit. They said they would think about it.

Four weeks later, I pulled up the stock quote and was shocked by the price per share. It had fallen back down to $6. I thought to myself, "I hope they sold close to the top."

Another couple of months went by. It was January now. Curious, I was wondering again what had happened to the investor's miracle stock. I checked and saw that it had fallen to below $3 per share. I called the investor and asked them what they ended up doing with their position.

Begrudgingly, the investor had said they had ridden the stock all the way up to $17 per share and then right back down to $3 per share. They admitted to being too paralyzed to do anything and were holding on in the hope that the stock would come back. They admitted to wishing they had placed those stop loss orders instead of watching the price plunge back down to earth. But they said that now that their account was back to where it was six months prior, they were just going to hang on for another couple years and see if it would make a comeback. I shook my head and wished them the best.

Three weeks later, the papers exploded with reports that the company was under investigation for fraud, and the stock price plummeted into the $1 per share range.

I think it goes without saying, but losing over $3.5 million over three to four months has to do something to your mental state. Had this investor implemented some of the tactics discussed in this chapter—sticking to a plan, managing risk, investing according to your personal rate of return, and so on—they likely would have avoided such a devastating loss.

This one experience altered how I work with clients in my private practice. Now, if I learn a client has unrealistic expectations or a pie-in-the-sky proclivity for reckless moves, I am very cautious about beginning a relationship. I would rather focus on building a steady and stable investment strategy that aligns with the goals outlined in the financial plan than chase returns. Those in the financial industry know that to live and die by performance alone means the client will consistently be frustrated with their status and wonder where they might be with a different investment strategy.

But miracle strategies don't exist. Many people are seduced by glittering tales (amplified by the sensationalistic financial media) of once-in-a-lifetime home runs on long-shot stock bets (e.g., bitcoin). What you usually don't hear about are the long-shot efforts that didn't pan out (or failed miserably). These against-the-odds triumphs are alluring, but they do not make for a savvy financial plan. Better to keep the gambling in Atlantic City.

CHAPTER 8

Where Did All My Money Go?: Tax Planning

To me, paying taxes feels like waiting for the rain after a long drought: You know it's coming but you don't know exactly how much it will be. Then, each year, around April 15, the skies break open and Uncle Sam dumps a bucket of cold water on your head.

I always go into my annual meeting with my accountant looking for more and more ways to ease the inevitable pain. And every year, I always wish there was a better way.

And maybe there is.

How Did We Get Here?

A brief history lesson is important to understand how we got here and what you should consider when building a "tax plan." Let's go back to a time when the nation was cleaved in two, in the throes of the Civil War. Prior to the war, the primary means of taxation was duties on goods like tobacco, carriages, sugar, and spirits. However, in 1861, to help finance the war effort and keep the country operational, Congress decided to pass the Revenue Act.[1] It was the first time the federal government imposed an income tax (a flat 3 percent rate) on the populace. The act was repealed a decade later.

A few decades later, in 1894, Congress again attempted to institute a flat tax system on personal income, but the Supreme Court ruled the tax unconstitutional the following year as the law did not allocate the tax by the populations of each state.[2] In a final attempt to tax personal income, in July 1909, Congress passed the Sixteenth Amendment, which allowed the government to tax personal income regardless of state population.[3] Eventually, in February 1913, the amendment was ratified, and the government has been taxing personal income ever since.

1 Ellen Terrell, "History of the US Income Tax," Library of Congress, 2012, http://www.loc.gov/rr/business/hottopic/irs_history.html.
2 Ibid.
3 "Brief History of IRS," Internal Revenue Service, https://www.irs.gov/about-irs/brief-history-of-irs.

Over the ensuing decades, tax rates continued to rise. Between the end of World War II and 1964, the highest marginal tax rate for the top 1 percent ranged approximately from 80 to 95 percent. Then in 1964, Congress passed another Revenue Act, which lowered all marginal rates. In 1981, President Ronald Regan, a strong proponent of "trickle-down economics," signed into law the Economic Recovery and Tax Act, which effected the largest tax cut since the 1960s by dropping marginal tax brackets, reducing the highest tax rate from 70 percent to 50 percent, reducing the lowest rate from 14 percent to 11 percent, slashing estate taxes, and trimming corporate taxes over a five-year period.[4]

Shortly after this law passed, there was an explosion in the federal deficit, relatively high unemployment, and mounting inflation, all of which caused short-term interest rates to spike from 12 percent to 20 percent. Between 1980 and 1982, the American economy entered into a double dip recession.[5]

U.S. Tax History at a Glance

Top federal marginal tax rate

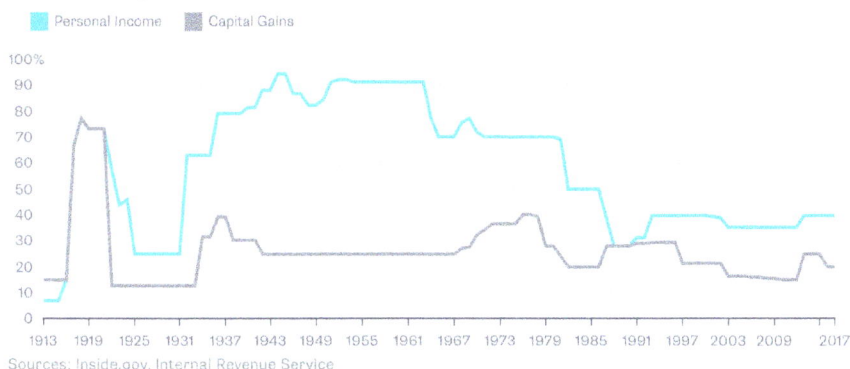

Sources: Inside.gov, Internal Revenue Service

---

4 Economic Recovery Tax Act, Pub.L. 97-34, 95 Stat. 172, 1981, http://www.legisworks. org/GPO/STATUTE-95-Pg172.pdf.
5 Tim Sablik, "Recession of 1982," Federal Reserve History, November 22, 2013, https://www.federalreservehistory.org/essays/recession_of_1981_82https://www. federalreservehistory.org/essays/recession_of_1981_82.

According to the reasoning behind trickle-down economics, tax cuts spark economic expansion, since if the government puts more money in the pockets of the American people and corporations, they'll spend more, which will in turn increase profitability and incentivize companies to grow, invest, and pay higher wages. In theory, that sounds pretty good. However, in the real world, this theory breaks down, as companies don't necessarily pass on their windfall to employees in the form of higher wages. The economic stimulus that trickle-down economics promises is usually short-lived, at best, if it happens at all.

Major tax cuts were enacted during the Reagan administration and the George W. Bush administration. How did GDP respond to these measures? According to the chart that follows, it would seem the economy experienced a pickup for the first couple of years. But later in each president's term, GDP returned to where it started, or even worsened. Now this does not necessarily mean the tax cuts issued during those times did not provide some help. However, they did not bring about the long-term expansion and economic growth that trickle-down advocates promised. And while there may have been other external factors that hindered long-term growth, the contention that tax cuts alone will spur economic growth is not necessarily true.

Real GDP Growth

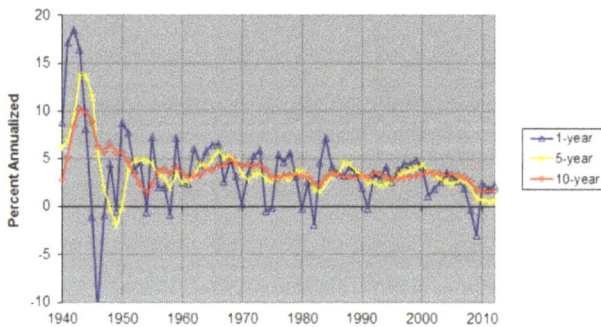

Source: http://www.bea.gov/national/xls/gdplev.xls

For decades, Wall Street has been complaining that the corporate tax rates are much too high as compared to those of the international community. While this is true in absolute terms, there are a ridiculous number of loopholes that allow corporations to lower their taxes below the official tax rate. The chart that follows shows that as a percentage of total federal revenues, individual tax receipts have stayed within a range of 40 percent to 50 percent over the last eighty years, even as the American population has grown. But the receipts from corporations over the same period have consistently declined. This suggests that individuals are shouldering an increasingly larger share of the tax burden.

So do tax cuts actually spur long-term expansion, or do they just provide temporary relief but enlarge the deficit, without delivering on their promised economic expansion? If total tax revenues stay flat

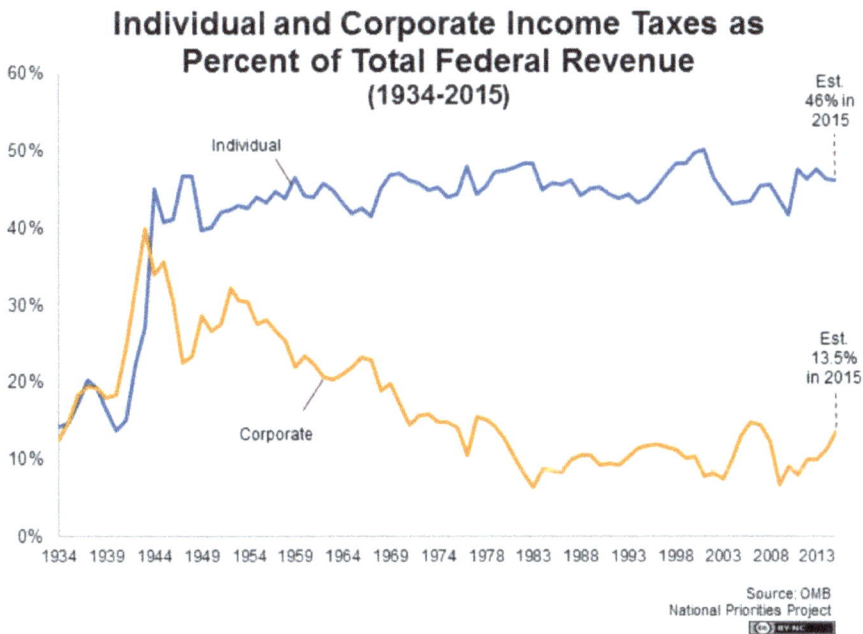

Individual and Corporate Income Taxes as Percent of Total Federal Revenue (1934-2015)

Source: OMB
National Priorities Project

or decline while government spending continues to climb, how will we ever balance our budget and pay off our mounting national debt? It seems fiscally reckless. And the financial planner in me balks at a scenario in which any entity—a person, a household, a corporation, or a government—is spending drastically more than it's bringing in.

Of course, you can perhaps make the case that the government cannot operate the way an individual household operates. There are too many issues to attend to, like various social responsibilities and national defense to think we can really maintain a balanced budget. But we're not just talking about a few dollars here and there of extra expenses. According to the Office of Management and Budget, in 2017, the federal government expected to spend over $400 billion more than it took in.[6] That ended up being a rather optimistic projection; by the end of the year, it ran a deficit of nearly $667 billion.[7] If we add the shortfall to our already massive $20 trillion dollar national debt,[8] we can quickly see how failing to balance the budget year after year can put us deep in the red.

"OK, Jonathan," you're thinking, "if I wanted to listen to a rant about the deficit, I'd schedule Thanksgiving early this year." I get it, but I'm not just soapboxing here. Rather, I want you to think about how Washington's (mis)management of the economy can impact your own financial situation. Will the government be forced to eventually raise taxes? Will we face another crippling recession in the near future?

---

6 "2017 United States Budget Estimate," InsideGov, http://federal-budget.insidegov.com/l/120/2017-Estimate.

7 Kate Davidson, "U.S. Ran $666 Billion Deficit In Fiscal 2017, Sixth Highest on Record," *Wall Street Journal*, Oct. 20, 2017, https://www.wsj.com/articles/u-s-ran-666-billion-deficit-in-fiscal-2017-sixth-highest-on-record-treasury-says-1508522722?mod=trending_now_4.

8 "U.S. Debt Clock," http://www.usdebtclock.org.

We're playing someone else's game, and we don't make the rules. But we can control how we move our pieces on the board. The next sections will show you how understanding the national tax situation can improve how you handle your personal tax situation.

Individual Tax and Capital Gains Tax Rates

As Ben Franklin is widely believed to have said,[9] only two things are guaranteed to us in life: death and taxes. Yet at least with death we do not have to worry about taxes anymore, and the sting of paying taxes might tempt some of us to choose an early death! Whatever your point of view is, the best we can do is prepare for both. To do that, we need to understand two types of taxes: ordinary income tax and capital gains tax.

Ordinary Income Tax

Whenever you hear people on television or in the newspaper talk about tax rates and whether they will go up or down, it is important to know they are generally talking about the "marginal tax rates," also known as "ordinary income tax rates." These are the progressive brackets each household is subject to based on its annual income. For example, in 2018, an individual or married couple whose adjusted gross income was $80,000 had a marginal bracket of 22 percent.[10]

Many people mistakenly think this 22 percent bracket means these households pay a tax of $17,600 (22 percent of $80,000). However,

---

9 Although Franklin did popularize this quote, he was not actually the one who coined the phrase, contrary to popular belief.

10 US Congress, H.R.1 - An Act to provide for reconciliation pursuant to titles II and V of the concurrent resolution on the budget for fiscal year 2018, accessed February 19, 2018: https://www.congress.gov/bill/115-congress/house-bill/1/text?q=%7B%22search%22%3A%5B.

that is not the case. Think of our current tax system as climbing a ladder that is broken into seven sections. As your income increases from $0 to $80,000, a portion of your total income will be taxed at the tax rate associated with each section (i.e., 10 percent, 12 percent, 22 percent, etc.). This means that you pay different tax rates for different portions of your income. As of this writing, for individual filers in 2018, the first $9,525 of income is taxed at the lowest rate. The 22 percent tax bracket applies only to income above $38,700 (but lower than $82,500). The total tax you pay is based on how many sections your total adjusted gross income falls into.

Let's lay this out using the previous example of $80,000. Instead of the individual or couple paying $80,000 × 22 percent = $17,600 in taxes, they instead pay this:

Individual: ($952.50 + $3,501 + $9,086) = **$13,539.50**
    ($9,525 × 10 percent) = $952.50
    ($38,700 − $9,525 = $29,175 × 12 percent) = $3,501
    ($80,000 − $38,700 = $41,300 × 22 percent) = $9,086

Couple: ($1,905 + $7,002 + $572) = **$9,479**
    ($19,050 × 10 percent) = $1,905
    ($77,400 − $19,050 = $58,350 × 12 percent) = $7,002
    ($80,000 − $77,400 = $2,600 × 22 percent) = $572

Now try this exercise with your income. Find out what your effective tax rate will be for this year. After performing the calculations and totaling up your taxes paid within each tax bracket, you will arrive at your "effective tax paid." This is actually how much you will pay in federal income tax based on your adjusted gross income. If you take the effective tax paid and divide it into your adjusted gross income, you'll get your "effective tax rate." In the example above the effective tax rates are 16.92 percent and 11.84 percent, respectively.

Every year the airwaves crackle with commentary about the marginal tax brackets, but few talk about the effective tax rate. I believe the media sensationalizes tax-related issues while doing a poor job of communicating what actually matters.

When we hear how marginal tax rates are going to stay the same or decline, we might think, "Whew, we dodged a bullet." However, that may not be the case. For example, when changes to the law reduce or eliminate the adjustments "above the line" that we can take to lower our income, then our "adjusted gross income" actually goes up, which makes our effective tax rate go up as well. Always stay abreast of such changes, and always make sure you know both your marginal tax bracket and your effective tax paid. Only then will you know how to build a tax plan for your future.

TIP

The previous section was a simplified example of marginal taxes. In reality we can lower our taxable income by claiming various deductions (i.e., standard or itemized). Some of us may even qualify for credits, which in many cases are better than deductions.

If you work with an accountant, then you will want to compare your prior year's tax liability with tax projections for the coming two years. This forecast can help you anticipate your future tax liability and determine whether there are any ways you can lower that upcoming tax. For example, if you can contribute an additional, deductible $5,000 to a retirement plan and your top marginal bracket is 22 percent, then you

---

have lowered your adjusted gross income by $5,000 and deferred paying $1,100 in taxes until you retire.

Capital Gains Tax

This type of tax is usually pretty straightforward, as it relates to the "capital gain or loss" from an investment. For example, if you purchase something for $10 and then sell it for $11, you are subject to a capital gains tax on the $1 gain. There are different rates for long-term and short-term capital gains depending on how long you held the investment before selling. In 2018, the long-term capital treatment was either 0 percent, 15 percent, or 20 percent, depending on what your adjusted gross income was for the year.[11]

When your holding period is less than one year, your gain, or loss, will be subject to a short-term capital gain, or loss, tax treatment—and taxed like ordinary income, as described in the previous section. On the other hand, if your holding period is longer than one year, your tax treatment is subject to long-term capital gain, or loss, treatment. (Though I hope you haven't been holding on to Beanie Babies since '97 in the hope they one day rebound. But then again, if you're invested in Beanie Babies, it's unlikely you'd be reading this book in the first place.)

Now that you understand ordinary income taxes, the effective tax, and the capital gains tax, let's look at how to integrate them to best assess how to manage your tax liability. To do this, I am going to illustrate another example.

---

11 "How Are Capital Gains Taxed?" Brookings Institution Tax Policy Center, Accessed February 19, 2018: http://www.taxpolicycenter.org/briefing-book/how-are-capital-gains-taxed

Imagine your household was filing MFJ (married filing jointly). The following is a very simple example of how you could build a tax plan to minimize the tax you owe.

	Scenario 1	Scenario 2
Gross Income	$95,000	$95,000
Retirement Plan Contributions	($1,000)	($10,000)
Long Term Capital Gains	$7,200	$16,200
Adjusted Gross Income	$101,200	$101,200
Standard Deductions	($24,000)	($24,000)
Taxable Income	$77,200	$77,200
Federal Tax Owed	$8,883	$8,883
Marginal Tax Bracket	12%	12%
Effective Tax	9.35%	9.35%
Capital Gains Savings	$1,080	$2,430

These are two fairly typical before-and-after scenarios. Focus your attention on the retirement contributions, the long-term capital gains, and the capital gains savings. Both scenarios attempt to eliminate the capital gains tax owed by keeping household income below the top end of the 12 percent marginal bracket, or $77,200. If it stays below this number, any capital gains upon sale of an investment would have zero capital gains tax liability, as the capital gains tax rate for a marginal tax bracket is 0 percent. It is important to note that the top end of the 12 percent bracket is $77,400, but the top end of the 15 percent capital gain bracket is $77,200.

Notice how both scenarios have the same taxable income and the same federal tax owed, but where they significantly differ is in how the household in Scenario 2 redirects savings from checking/spending into their retirement plan, thus reducing the impact on their capital gains tax liability. By electing to contribute an additional $9,000 to their employer-sponsored plan, instead of paying the tax on the $9,000 and putting what is left over in savings, Scenario 2 allows the household to rebalance (buy and sell) a larger portion of their investment portfolio, which in turn allows them to realize a larger portion of the capital gains. The larger rebalance allows the household to save an *additional* $1,350 in capital gains tax because they will remain in the 12 percent marginal tax bracket where the capital gains rate is 0 percent.

So why is this important? In the last chapter, we talked about the importance of managing the risk in your portfolio. If you have been investing for any significant length of time, your investment portfolio surely has some unrealized gains. These gains will create some imbalance within your portfolio and you will be required to rebalance the accounts in order to keep your asset allocation the way you want. Therefore, rebalancing a nonqualified investment account will subject you to capital tax treatment, which could affect your annual taxable income. It is important to note that pretax, qualified retirement accounts are not subject to a capital gains tax like nonqualified brokerage accounts, but I will explain that issue in the next section.

Now if that was all Greek to you, that is OK. Just know that what you do with your portfolios can have a direct impact on the tax bracket you end up in at the end of a year. I have seen clients rebalance portfolios without an understanding of their tax burden and the result catapulted them into another marginal tax bracket and subjected them to the alternative minimum tax (and in some cases the net investment income tax). The bottom line, in order not to get hosed in taxes by our neighborhood friends at the Internal Revenue Service, managing your capital tax treatment will become increasingly important as your portfolio grows in size.

To Qualify or Not to Qualify?

Now that you understand two of the most common taxes Americans are subject to annually, we need to turn our attention to the vehicles into which we can save money and ideally shelter money from the government.

Qualified Accounts

A qualified employer retirement account is an employer-sponsored retirement plan that gets special tax treatment in accord with Section 401(a) of the Internal Revenue Code. These accounts have been around since the 1970s, but the general concept was born a long time before that.

In 1875, American Express had the idea of creating an account that a company would contribute to on behalf of their employees in order to offer an incentive for workers and promote employee loyalty. And thus the first pension plan was born.[12] The idea caught on, and in 1921, the Revenue Act decreed that pension plans would become the first qualified plan to shelter taxable income from taxation while employees were employed.

Later, the concept of a tax shelter expanded beyond defined benefit plans (where the employer makes the sole contribution) to defined

---

12 Jeffrey Lehman and Shirelle Phelps, eds., "Pension," *West's Encyclopedia of American Law, 2nd Ed.,* (Boston: Gale Cengage, 2005).

contributions plans (where the employee and employer make contributions). The Revenue Act of 1978 created qualified accounts as a way to allow Americans to shelter their income. These accounts were a welcome reprieve from the astronomically high tax rates of the late '70s, and they allowed investors to defer paying taxes on their earnings. Today, most American use qualified accounts in the form of the 401(k), 403(b), thrift savings plans, or Individual Retirement Accounts.

Nonqualified Accounts

Unlike qualified accounts that defer the tax liability to a future date, nonqualified accounts are subject to ordinary tax and capital tax treatment in the year the income or gain is realized. Examples of these accounts are investment brokerage accounts, checking accounts, savings accounts, certificates of deposit, and many more. Therefore, selecting the right investments and periodically rebalancing them becomes increasingly important each and every year. Otherwise, as noted in previous sections of this chapter, you could end up needlessly enlarging your tax liability.

Which Is Better?

With a baseline understanding of the two types of accounts, you can ask, "Where do you think you should save your money first?" If you are like most of my clients, you might say the qualified accounts because contributions there lower your current year tax liability whereas nonqualified accounts can increase current year tax liability.

Now let's ask a different question: "When do you think you will be in a lower tax bracket, now or later?" Most of my clients presume they'll be in a lower tax bracket in the future, thinking that their earnings while they're employed will be significantly higher than when they're retired.

On its face, this makes sense. But what if they're wrong?

Consider this scenario: You and your spouse are both working, making at least $140,000 combined per year. Based on the current marginal tax rates, you fall in the 22 percent bracket. Both of you save $10,000 into your respective retirement plans per year. You also pay for health insurance with pretax dollars to the tune of $3,000 each year. These contributions are considered above the adjusted gross income (AGI) line and drop your AGI to $117,000. So far you are still in the 22 percent marginal bracket, but after doing some math you find that your effective tax rate has declined because you have reduced your AGI. All seems right with the world.

Time ticks on. Both of you continue to thrive in your careers, and your combined income increases to $225,000. You're both elated that you're now making more money than you ever have in your life. As your incomes increase, you start to save more, but soon you realize that you are also paying more in taxes, because at approximately $165,000 of income, you jumped into the 24 percent marginal bracket.

To help reduce the tax bite, you increase your contributions to your retirement plans to max funding levels. In 2018, the maximum 401(k) contribution was $18,500 per person. Therefore, together, you are saving a combined $37,000. At the same time you are still paying for health insurance but the cost has increased to $5,000 annually.

After all pretax deductions, you find that your AGI is now $183,000, which means that even after all the extra saving into the qualified accounts, your marginal tax bracket is still 24 percent.

This cycle of income growth continues on for another twenty years, and you continue to look for ways to save as much as you can into your pretax accounts.

Finally, the day arrives when you retire. Both of you have done an amazing job of saving and growing your money—after all, you've been saving $37,000 into your retirement plans for about twenty-five years, averaging an annual 6.5 percent return (compounded monthly). You have amassed nearly $2.3 million dollars in your retirement accounts. These dollars *plus* whatever you saved into your nonqualified accounts *plus* any pensions *plus* Social Security will be what you use to live on in retirement.

If we conservatively estimate that you withdraw $81,000 from your qualified accounts (or 3.5 percent of your balance) annually, you have a small pension that pays $10,000 per year, and you will each collect $25,000 per year in Social Security at full-retirement age, then your total taxable income (not including any deductions) would be $141,000 per year. Using today's marginal tax rates, that puts you back in the 22 percent marginal tax bracket. This demonstrates that it's faulty to *assume* your retirement income tax bracket will be significantly lower than your preretirement income tax bracket.

Moreover, don't assume that the marginal tax rates won't go up, even if the 2017 tax law decreased them. If the national debt is already above $20 trillion and continues to climb, how long will it be before the government is forced to raise taxes to address fears about the country's insolvency? If this happens (and it's certainly a plausible scenario), wouldn't it make more sense to pay taxes in the lower marginal rates now than at some date in the future?

Thinking through the answers to these questions can help you create a better tax plan for how you save, invest, and grow your money over time.

Pulling It All Together: Tax Location

Whew! Are you ready to throw in the towel yet? Taxes will make your head hurt when you begin to dig into some of the intricacies and then try to extrapolate the possibilities for your future.

Now, you need to think about where to invest your dollars to maximize your opportunity for growth and minimize the tax hit. This is where we get into the discussion of "tax location." Tax location is the process by which an investor reallocates their investments across all of their accounts to minimize the realization of taxable dividends annually.

This was a simple concept that was first explained to me early in my career and is something many of my clients struggle with as they build their investment strategy. To create a tax location strategy, you need to know which investments in your account generate ordinary dividends (fixed income, like bonds) and qualified dividends (equities, like domestic stocks). Then you look at your accounts and determine how much money you have in qualified accounts versus nonqualified accounts. From there you begin to allocate more of your ordinary dividend–producing investments to qualified accounts in order to defer the taxes on those distributions. Finally, you need to evaluate the risk/return trade-off of each investment in the corresponding account and determine if you are comfortable with one account having a slower growth rate than the others due to their higher weighting to fixed income.

TIP

If you borrow on margin in your nonqualified account and intend to deduct the investment interest expense, make sure you do not have any qualified dividends. Those that deduct investment interest expenses, like margin interest, are required to convert – dollar for dollar–the qualified dividends into ordinary dividends. This means the qualified

---

dividends lose their 15 percent preferential tax status and are taxed at your ordinary tax rate,[13] which could be as high as 37 percent in 2018.

It is important to understand that while some accounts may have slower growth potential than other accounts, it is the overall asset mix across all accounts that is really what counts. The individual accounts you use are the mechanisms by which you select the investments. In other words, the accounts you use are the starting point for selecting certain investments that are more appropriately suited for the tax preference of the account.

Essentially, designing a tax location strategy involves these tasks:

1. Finding your free cash flow (chapter 3)
2. Outlining your financial goals (chapter 3)
3. Finding your savings rate (chapter 5)
4. Finding your required rate of return, or personal rate of return (chapter 5)
5. Assessing your risk profile (chapter 7)
6. Creating an asset allocation mix that matches your risk profile and targets your personal rate of return (chapter 7)

To put it together you need to follow this funneling approach:

1. Start with an overall target asset allocation goal.
2. Determine what types of accounts you have to use (qualified vs. nonqualified).

---

13 C. Andrew Lafond, CPA, DBA, and Jeffrey J. Schrader, CPA, MST, "Don't neglect to elect, part 4," *Journal of Accountancy*, January 31, 2013: https://www.journalofaccountancy.com/issues/2013/feb/20126851.html

3. Calculate how much money, as a percentage of the whole, resides in qualified accounts vs. nonqualified ones.

4. Determine what percentage of your fixed income holdings should be allocated to your qualified accounts.

5. Allocate the remaining asset classes between your qualified accounts and nonqualified accounts to meet your target level of realized ordinary dividends.

6. As you save money monthly, contribute money in the same manner and allocation as the rest of your portfolio. You do not want to increase your asset classes in the wrong account and run the risk of increasing ordinary dividends in future years while also increasing your risk with riskier assets.

Let's walk through a hypothetical example involving a target allocation of 50 percent equities and 50 percent fixed income. The assets total $100,000, with $40,000 in nonqualified accounts and $60,000 in qualified accounts. The goal is to minimize ordinary dividends. In the nonqualified account(s), invest $25,000 in equities, $10,000 in tax-free bonds, and $5,000 in taxable bonds. Then in the qualified account(s), invest $25,000 in equities and $35,000 in taxable bonds. The income produced in the qualified accounts is sheltered by the tax-deferred nature of the qualified accounts.

Note that this example is for anyone not in the 10 percent or 12 percent tax brackets, as the after-tax yield of tax-free bonds does not meet that of taxable bonds. Before rebalancing, the investor needs to assess the tax liability in the nonqualified account(s) associated with the unrealized gains. If there are large unrealized gains, the rebalance may take time.

Of all the chapters in this book, this is certainly one of the most complicated to understand. If you had a hard time following along, it might help you to know I had a hard time writing it. It's easier to explain it to a client face-to-face, where I can break each concept down and help them understand by applying the principles to their own portfolio. It also helps if I can draw pictures in person to better illustrate my points.

The main takeaway is this: Building a tax plan as part of your overall financial plan is vitally important, as it can offer significant benefits to you today and for many years to come. This is something that goes beyond the normal scope of, say, an accountant. While accountants are great at what they do, most of them do not focus on the *future*, which means their clients are missing a lot of the concepts outlined in this chapter. If you want to maximize loopholes, accountants are a great resource. If you want to minimize future tax liability, make sure you understand what you read in this chapter, or work with a planner who understands your life, your goals, and how to build a tax plan that can change as you and your financial situation change over time.

TIP

Look at the first page of your tax return—Form 1040—and look at lines 8a, 8b, 9a, and 9b. This is where you can find your taxable interest and dividends. By shifting interest income from line 8a to 8b and dividend income from 9a to 9b, you can save thousands in taxes. I have implemented this strategy numerous times and have deferred or eliminated thousands of dollars in taxes owed every year—*legally*. If you learn nothing else from this book, make sure you understand the concept of tax location.

CHAPTER 9

More Than Just Will: Estate Planning

Today, as I write this, it happens to be Thanksgiving. We have a tradition in our household, one that many of you probably do as well, where we think back on the year and list what we accomplished, what and whom we are thankful for, and what we want to accomplish before the end of the year.

As I sit here in the soft glow of my living room lamp, listening to the kids playing in the next room, I feel like I am having one of those television flashbacks. As the flashback fades in, I think about the struggles of starting another company, my attempt to write a book, how I added another five letters to the end of my business card with another certification, and a bunch of other things. I realize I achieved much more this year than in any previous year, and much of that wouldn't have happened without those in my life who supported my endeavors, like my clients, my friends, and most importantly, my family.

As the flashback fades out, I realize there is one task I have yet to do. And it happens to be one that, if left unfinished, would cause my family a lot of heartache.

So as I lay out what needs to happen over the next four weeks, I send some emails to a few friends to see who can fit me in to update some documents for me. I haven't updated my estate documents in quite a while. Everything that has happened in my life—everything I've achieved—means little if I don't protect what I have worked so hard to build, for the benefit of my family.

The Purpose of Estate Planning

I think we all intuitively know we need a plan for "what happens next" in the event of a catastrophe, yet many of us do not heed this voice of caution. Countless individuals and couples I've worked with over the years say they put it off because they're "too busy," or because of "the amount of work involved." And it does indeed involve a fair amount of work. Yet having a contingency plan helps reduce the disruption in your life and the lives of your loved ones.

To plan accordingly, you must answer a lot of if-then questions. For instance, if you were in a car accident tomorrow and ended up in a coma, who would step in to make your medical decisions? Would the same person be in charge of your financial affairs? Such questions are emotionally fraught and all point to a hard question: "Whom do you trust with your most important matters?"

Most people would name their spouse or a family member. But if that person wasn't available, would you have a friend whom you could implicitly trust, like family, with such an immense responsibility? These kinds of weighty questions make us take a hard look at our relationships and ask whether the people we hang out with are true friends or just drinking buddies.

If you've been putting off estate planning, or if it's never really crossed your mind, this chapter will steer you on the right course. We can break down estate planning into a core set of documents that everyone should have: a will, an advanced medical directive or living will, a power of attorney, a letter of intent, and in some cases a trust or two.

The Rules for Passing Assets

There are three processes you need to understand that concern how you transfer assets to a beneficiary: **outright**, via a **will**, and via a **trust**. Each option offers certain advantages and disadvantages.

Outright

When you open an account (checking account, brokerage account, etc.), you usually have to name a "beneficiary." When you created your balance sheet back in chapter 3, did you think about who would receive those assets in the event you died? Probably not. That's OK. Most of my clients either do not remember who they selected or never selected anyone in the first place. However, the decision is an important one, because when you croak, the assets will be distributed "outright" either to your beneficiary or to your estate.

When it comes to selecting a beneficiary, banks and investment firms take a similar approach; however, each applies a different label to the process. For banks, the process is known as "pay on death." This means that when the personal representative of your estate (i.e., your executor or executrix) informs your bank that you have died, the bank will proceed to freeze the account and work with the personal representative to locate the beneficiary listed on the account so the assets in that account can be transferred directly to the beneficiary, instead of going through the process of probate.

For investment firms, there are two distinct processes for selecting beneficiaries. The first is known as "transfer on death" and applies to nonqualified investment accounts. This process is nearly identical to the process outlined by the bank. The second applies to qualified accounts like IRAs and employer-sponsored plans. This process is known as a "beneficiary designation" and simply requires you to list a beneficiary on the account. Like the pay on death, both the transfer on death and the beneficiary designation allow the beneficiaries to avoid going through the probate process, which can be complicated and costly.

In each of these three methods (pay on death, transfer on death, and beneficiary designation), your cash and investments are left directly to a named beneficiary, are difficult to contest after death because they are not probated, supersede the wishes outlined in a will, and provide the beneficiaries with quick access to their inheritance. The streamlined nature of these methods is an advantage.

However, there are two major drawbacks. The first is in cases where the beneficiary is a minor. Every state agrees that minors are not able to make legal or financial decisions before the age of majority, typically eighteen, though in some cases twenty-one. Therefore, minor children named as beneficiaries will not be able to receive their assets until they come of age. To facilitate this transfer, when there is no named guardian, the courts will appoint a "guardian ad litem" whose sole job is to investigate which solutions would be in the best interest of the child. In many cases I have seen, the court-appointed representative acts as the child's financial guardian and manages the assets until they turn eighteen. If that sounds easy, it is not. This person doesn't know your child but is responsible for their financial well-being. Oh, and they charge an ongoing fee until their services are no longer needed.

Alternatively, when there *is* an appointed guardian of the child, the courts may appoint that person to control the child's inherited financial assets. In some cases, like if the guardian is your ex-spouse, there is a cause for concern that the assets will be used for the benefit of the guardian's lifestyle rather than the child's.

The second drawback to naming someone outright has to do with the concern over trusting an eighteen-year-old to be a good steward of a potentially vast inheritance. Think back to when you were eighteen: How many of you would have been able to make intelligent financial decisions about your future when a five-, six-, or seven-figure bank account was suddenly thrust into your hands? Even some adults would struggle with the massive responsibility and need for restraint this entails. We hope our children are able to make the right choice, but it is usually hard to know for sure. Consequently, many attorneys recommend placing the assets in a trust for the benefit of the child until an age after eighteen, like twenty-one, twenty-five, or thirty, depending on the child's financial acumen.

Whatever your choice is for naming a beneficiary, I always encourage clients to review their beneficiary designations at least annually to ensure the right people are named. The last thing you want is your ex-spouse to receive what your new spouse *should* have received. Or for your criminally delinquent, drug-prone heir to use the funds to further their destructive habits. Or for your well-meaning but errant twenty-year-old to sink your life savings into an ill-conceived musical comedy web series. You get the picture.

Dying Intestate

If you do not have any estate planning documents in place today and have not named outright beneficiaries of your possessions, at your death you will most likely be considered to have died "intestate"—the legal term for not having made a will before death.

The law varies by state, but in Virginia, where I live and work, if you are married and pass away without a will, your assets will be passed on to your spouse as follows:[1]

- All assets go to the surviving spouse, unless there are children (or their descendants) of someone other than the surviving spouse, in which case one-third goes to the surviving spouse and the remaining two-thirds are divided among all children.

- If there is no surviving spouse, all passes to the children and their descendants (see "outright" drawbacks 1 and 2 above).

- If none, all goes to the deceased's father and mother or the survivor.

- If none, all passes to the deceased's brothers and sisters and their descendants.

In Virginia, the path by which assets transfer is fairly simple except in the case of a second marriage. If your intent was to leave your current spouse of thirty years with a generous nest egg to provide them a comfortable retirement, they could be in for a rude awakening when it comes time to settle the estate and two-thirds of your financial assets are left to the children of your previous marriage. This happens more often than you might think.

Therefore, I encourage you to review your state's intestacy laws if you do not have a will, to ensure your assets pass as you intend. Otherwise, I recommend investing in a will to make sure your assets reach their intended destination.

---

1 "Probate in Virginia," Virginia Court Clerks' Association, 2015, http://www.courts.state.va.us/courts/circuit/resources/probate_in_virginia.pdf.

Dying with a Will

If your state's laws do not encourage the optimal outcome for how your assets pass after you die, you probably want a will. A will, in most cases, is simply a set of instructions that tell the person in charge of your estate (the executor or executrix) how to distribute your final assets after they have taken a tally of your estate. However, a will can be much more than a simple list of instructions. When drafted correctly, a will can create a long-standing legacy by outlining instructions for how your estate will be handled through a mechanism like a testamentary trust (which I explain later in this chapter).

So what does a will really help with? Well, more often than not, when someone dies, their estate will be required to go through the process of probate. In fact, the probate of a will means to prove its genuineness in probate court. *West's Encyclopedia of American Law* states:

"Unless otherwise provided by statute, a will must be admitted to probate before a court will allow the distribution of a decedent's property to the heirs according to its terms.

As a general rule, a will has no legal effect until it is probated. A will should be probated immediately, and no one has the right to suppress it. The person with possession of a will, usually the personal representative or the decedent's attorney, must produce it. Statutes impose penalties for concealing or destroying a will or for failing to produce it within a specified time.

To qualify as a will in probate, an instrument must be of testamentary character and comply with all statutory requirements. A document is testamentary when it does not take effect until after the death of the person making it and allows the individual to retain the property under personal control during her or his lifetime. A will that has been properly executed by a competent person—the testator—as required by law is entitled to be probated, even if some of its provisions are invalid, obscure, or cannot be implemented."[2]

The word *competent* in the last sentence of this lengthy description hints at something even more interesting, and possibly nefarious. If it can be proven that the testator did not have "testamentary capacity," then the document could be held unenforceable. Furthermore, individuals who might be unhappy with how the assets are distributed can contest the will, drawing into question the language of the document, the intent of the deceased, and the named beneficiaries. Anyone who believes they are entitled to the inheritance can contest the will. All they have to do is file a petition with the court in the state of the decedent and state their case with supporting evidence. A lien holder, an old coworker, a disgruntled family member, or pretty much anyone else can contest someone's will on almost any grounds. The court will decide the validity of the claim and award accordingly.

This calls attention to the fact that wills can act as a mechanism for distribution, but they are not free from complications, which makes using them for large estates a risky decision. In that case, using a trust may make more sense.

Dying with a Trust

You might be thinking, "I don't want a stranger controlling my kids' assets or having someone contest my will." In that case, there is one other place you can turn: a trust.

---

2 *West's Encyclopedia of American Law, Second Ed.,* (Farmington Hills, MI: The Gale Group, Inc., 2008).

In my professional opinion, a trust provides additional protections beyond simply estate tax protection, though after the 2017 Tax Cut and Jobs Act, your personal estate would need to exceed $11.2 million for a single person or $22.4 million for a married couple before any federal estate tax would be levied against the estate. If you're unconcerned with "creditors, predators, in-laws, and outlaws," there is limited need for a trust. But if you are worried about an heir mismanaging their inheritance, or about people finding out about your heir's sudden wealth, or if you want to keep your money in the bloodline and out of the hands of a current in-law *or* future "outlaw," then a trust provides specific benefits to you and your family that cannot be realized through a simple will.

When I start any estate planning discussion with a client, I make sure they understand I am not an attorney and the advice I give is based on my education, experience, and understanding of the law. It should not be taken as a replacement for working with an attorney.

Once that's out of the way, I ask the client a series of questions to better understand their goals and fears. One common question is, "What happens to my money once I am dead?" In fact, after we have gone through the discussion on how to leave assets to heirs that I included in this chapter, they usually ask, "What do I do to keep our money in our family?"

That is when I explain the concept of trust planning and the various roles involved.

Parties to a Trust

When setting up a trust, there are four parties you need to be aware of: the grantor, the trustee, the successor trustee, and the beneficiary.

The *grantor, or settlor,* of any trust is typically the person who funds the trust—namely, you. A trust can be established by the grantor or by a third party. A third party may establish a trust on the grantor's behalf in certain cases, such as those involving minors, or incapacitation.

The *trustee* of your trust typically starts off being you and potentially your spouse depending on how your trust is set up. This allows you to maintain control over your assets during your life, and is no different than having your account titled solely in your name or in joint name with someone else.

The *successor trustee* is your replacement. In case you cannot fulfill the duties specified in your trust, this person steps in and controls the assets of the trust in accordance with the language in the trust document. A successor trustee usually assumes this role if you are incapacitated or cannot, willfully or legally, act on your own behalf. Usually, it's the next of kin who steps in, but sometimes it can be a financial institution.

The *beneficiary* is the person, or entity, who will receive the benefits associated with the trust. During life you will most likely be the grantor, the trustee, and the beneficiary of your trust.

In many cases, at the death of the grantor, when assets are titled in trust, the successor trustee will follow the language of the trust and either pass the assets on directly to the beneficiary or leave the assets in the trust, with the beneficiary receiving distributions over a period of time.

Revocable versus Irrevocable

While there are multiple types of trusts that accomplish all sort of tasks, here, we'll highlight the basics of trust planning and explore two common types of trusts: **revocable** and **irrevocable trusts**.

As the name suggests, a revocable trust permits the owner of the trust to revoke or change any element of the trust language while they have capacity to do so. This type of trust acts as an extension of you, in a way similar to that of an individual or joint account registration.

The primary difference in asset transfer between a trust, a will, and an outright transfer is what happens at death. In an outright transfer or transfer by will, the asset's title and ownership is changed from your name to the beneficiary's name. Yet when an asset is titled in a revocable trust, the trust is actually the owner of the asset and you are the signatory. At death, the asset stays in trust until the trustee, or successor trustee, either distributes all the assets or until the trust dissolves by operation of law.

Finally upon your death, your trust changes from being revocable to being irrevocable. This means the ability to change the language in the trust ends at the grantor's death. Therefore whatever is written into the trust becomes "the law of the trust" and cannot be altered without a court intervening. An example of when the court would intervene might be when, say, a trust is set to dissolve on the fifth anniversary of the grantor's death, but the trustee feels the beneficiaries are not mentally ready to inherit the contents of the trust.

Trust Planning Protects More Than Money

There are three primary advantages of using a trust during life.

1. Titling assets in your trust during life means that at your death, assets titled in the trust will not be subject to the probate process, similar to an outright transfer as mentioned above. This makes the transfer of any asset owned by the trust a private transaction that is not open to public view. In contrast, the

probate process, since it's handled by the courts, can reveal more than you might be comfortable with. Just do a Google search for Jacqueline Kennedy Onassis. You can read all about how her estate was valued between $43 million and $73 million, who received which properties, and how charitable lead trusts were used to pass money on to the grandkids.[3]

2. A trust can allow for the distribution of assets over an extended period, sometimes in perpetuity, depending on your state's laws. This is how assets can be passed down from one generation to another without the beneficiaries ever taking ownership. In practical terms, think of how the John D. Rockefeller Trust and Foundation pays income to Rockefeller's heirs. Assets are held in the trust and a portion of the income is paid out annually to all of the beneficiaries. As the trust reaches the end of its legal lifetime, one trust is closed by the trustee, with the court's approval, and another is opened based on the powers and the trust language outlined in the document.

Irrevocable trusts, when written correctly, can offer protection from outsiders who may be looking to attack the assets.

Fundamentally, trusts provide "control" from beyond the grave in order to protect your family from themselves and from outsiders. Therefore, as you undertake the if-then line of questioning, ask yourself what your vision for your assets is. Do you feel your heirs are responsible enough to spend what took you decades to earn? There is nothing wrong with wanting to protect your family's interests, even if that means protecting them from themselves.

---

3 David Cay Johnston, "Mrs. Onassis's Estate Worth Less Than Estimated," *New York Times,* December 21, 1996, http://www.nytimes.com/1996/12/21/nyregion/mrs-onassis-s-estate-worth-less-than-estimated.html.

This section is just an overview of trust planning. Addressing all the nuances (not to mention all the jurisdiction-specific points of law) would take fifty more pages, if not an entire book. The point is to help you understand how your assets will pass from you to a future heir (and whether the IRS gets a cut, via taxes, as well). For more in-depth planning tailored to your particular circumstance, talk to a financial planner and an attorney who specializes in estate planning.

Some attorneys believe a **testamentary trust** (or trust created out of a will) is better than a standalone trust, because it simplifies the estate. Yet a testamentary trust is only really created after death, which means the assets of an individual pass through probate before arriving in a testamentary trust, thus making your estate a matter of public record, similar to Jackie Onassis'. This seems counterintuitive if your goal is to avoid probate. If you decide a trust is best for you, you can set it up now and make small adjustments over future decades.

Nervous yet...? Well I have some additional goodies to share with you that might fill your britches.

Incapacity

It is unnerving to watch people plan for the future, thinking they'll die before they end up incapacitated when, in fact, we have a higher probability of being incapacitated before we die. To plan for this scenario, you need two documents in place that will give those around you direction on how to think and act when you are unable: a power of attorney, and a living will, or Advanced Medical Directive.

A Power of Attorney

Earlier I posed to you a question: Whom do you trust implicitly? Did you come up with an answer? If you did, this person might be a great stand-in when you are no longer able to oversee your legal and financial affairs. The term for such a person is "attorney-in-fact." But just informally telling them they are in charge doesn't mean they have the authority to act on your behalf. Instead, they need a document—a power of attorney—that spells out exactly what they are and are not allowed to do.

The Legal Information Institute at Cornell formally defines a power of attorney as "an agreement between two parties: a principal and an attorney-in-fact. The attorney-in-fact need not be an attorney at law (a lawyer). A power of attorney gives the attorney-in-fact rights to act in the principal's place. Attorneys in fact are fiduciaries of their principals."[4]

If the choice between "doing" and "delegating" underlies every aspect of the financial blueprint presented in this book, then bestowing someone with a power of attorney is the ultimate "delegation." It is not to be taken lightly. But which power of attorney do you give them? In the complicated world of estate planning, there are three power of attorney documents you should know about.

General, or Durable, Power of Attorney

The most far-reaching of the three, this document allows your appointed person to make decisions about your financial and sometimes medical affairs the moment you sign the document into existence. Furthermore, this document stays in effect even if you are incapacitated.

When electing to draft this type of document, you need to make sure the person you name is someone you trust completely. Don't overlook this point—I have seen horror stories when the wrong

---

4 Legal Information Institute, "Power of Attorney," https://www.law.cornell.edu/wex/power_of_attorney.

person is given authority over someone's most intimate concerns. For example, I worked with an elderly client who was living in independent housing. She was taking care of herself quite well and was very self-sufficient. She had a son, but she had purposefully not added him to her investment or bank accounts as a cosignatory because she was worried that his money problems would somehow spill over onto her.

When she developed health problems, she was encouraged by her attorney to give her son a durable power of attorney. Although she knew he had financial troubles, she wanted to give him the benefit of the doubt, and in any case, she needed him around more now than ever.

Six months went by and she floated in and out of the hospital, becoming more and more reliant on him. Eventually, he took over all of her finances. It was at that time he decided to move her accounts to another institution under the rationale that "it was for her benefit."

Suspicious, I performed a little detective work and looked through the transaction history of the accounts to which she had given me access (since I was her financial advisor). I saw that her once-pristine statements had been sullied with random odd credit card and bank account charges over the past half a year. At first, the charges were intermittent and small, but by the time he was moving her accounts, the "one-off transactions" had become more regular and larger. Sadly, all I could do was report it to my compliance department, which would conduct its own investigation, but beyond that it was unclear what more they could do. After the accounts left my financial institution, all contact with my client and her son ceased. I never got to learn what happened to them.

Just because you trust someone today doesn't mean they will be 100 percent trustworthy in the future. If you elect to give someone a power of attorney, make sure you know them inside and out. Performing periodic "check-ins" with the pick for your replacement ranks right up there in order of importance with saying "I do" at your wedding, calling an attorney after you win the lottery, and eating healthy to avoid diabetes and heart disease.

Springing Power of Attorney

Similar to the general power of attorney, this document does grant access to operate your life on your behalf but is *not* enforceable from the moment you walk out of your attorney's office. Instead, this document has a clause that says something to this effect: "In the event you are incapacitated as noted and approved by one, or two, attending physicians, then the person named in your power of attorney steps in."

This document requires you to explicitly spell out what the "springing" provision is, what triggers the provision, and the types of powers this document bestows upon your attorney-in-fact.[5] The purpose of this document is to make sure you are truly incapacitated based on those provisions before someone takes control of your life decisions. The downside is that the more stringent standard of what constitutes "incapacitation" might take extra time to confirm; therefore, there could be a lag time between when you become incapacitated and when your agent is able to make decisions on your behalf.

Limited Power of Attorney

In this last version you can break down who does what, assigning specific duties to specific people. If you want one person to act as

---

5 Amelia Granger, "Springing v. Durable Power of Attorney," NerdWallet, June 26, 2012, https://www.nerdwallet.com/blog/investing/estate-planning/springing-durable-power-attorney/.

your attorney-in-fact for health-care decisions and another to act as attorney-in-fact for financial decisions, then you can have two separate documents that spell out the rules for each. Additionally, if you were to put one person in charge of your health-care decisions and another in charge of your finances, you could give the former the durable health-care power of attorney and for the latter use a springing financial power of attorney. This way, the person who needs to make medical decisions can do so even if you're not classified as incapacitated, whereas the other would be required to obtain a doctor's letter, or two, in order to gain control over your finances.

As you might expect, every state has different rules over different power of attorney documents. Some may not accept or acknowledge one version or may refer to these documents by different names. Regardless of the legal and jurisdictional specifics, one thing is always true: whomever you name as your stand-in, make sure you trust them *totally—and* make sure you trust their replacement in the event they resign or cannot perform their duties as specified in the document.

One last thing to consider here: Adult children eighteen to thirty-five years of age need to have these documents in place too, if they don't already. Otherwise their parents will have a very hard time acting on their child's behalf. For example, a college student suffers a serious accident, but the parents do not have the power to make medical decisions because the child is nineteen.

Living Will, or Advanced Medical Directive

Simply stated, this document tells your doctors and your attorney-in-fact what you want your final hours, days, or weeks to look like. It can spell out whether you want your organs donated to others or to science, or preserved in a jar to spook your grandkids on Halloween (note: may or may not be legal in your jurisdiction). It can outline your religious beliefs and what should happen to your body when you die. Most importantly of all, this document tells your loved ones what your wishes are if you are in a vegetative state, like a coma. One of the most agonizing decisions someone can face in life is whether to pull the plug or give their loved one one more day in the hope that they come out of a coma.

One particularly wrenching case you may be familiar with was that of Terri Schiavo. It was a case in which one family's personal, private decision about whether to resuscitate became a polarizing nationwide controversy. While Terri's case was unique, similar disputes play out all across the country, every day.

For fifteen years, Terri was hooked up to life support while her husband squared off with her family members over whether to continue the treatment or end her life. Terri herself had left no written instructions, so it was impossible to determine what she would have wanted.

Based on the doctors' diagnosis of a "persistent vegetative state" from which she had no hope of recovering, and spoken statements she had made in the past about not wanting to "be kept alive on a machine," Michael wanted his wife removed from life support.[6] The Schindler family refused to accept the doctors' diagnosis and fought bitterly with Michael. "Thus began wide-ranging, acrimonious legal and public-opinion battles that eventually involved multiple special-interest groups who saw this case as a cause célèbre for their particular

---

6 Timothy E. Quill, "Terri Schiavo—A Tragedy Compounded," *New England Journal of Medicine*, 352 (April 21, 2005): 1630-1633, http://www.nejm.org/doi/full/10.1056/NEJMp058062#t=article.

issue," wrote Dr. Timothy Quill in the *New England Journal of Medicine*. "The story of Terri Schiavo should be disturbing to all of us. How can it be that medicine, ethics, law, and family could work so poorly together in meeting the needs of this woman who was left in a persistent vegetative state after having a cardiac arrest?"[7]

I often ask clients about their understanding of a living will. The typical response highlights the fact that many people confuse a living will with a "do not resuscitate" (DNR) order. The two are related, but not the same. A DNR is a medical order written by a doctor. It instructs health-care providers not to do cardiopulmonary resuscitation (CPR) if a patient's breathing stops or if the patient's heart stops beating. A DNR order is created, or set up, before an emergency occurs. A DNR order allows you to choose whether or not you want CPR in an emergency. It is specific about CPR. It does not have instructions for other treatments, such as pain medicine, other medicines, or nutrition."[8]

This means that in addition to a living will and all of the other documents previously discussed, you need to decide if you want a DNR added to the list.

Letter of Intent

This is one of the documents that attorneys often overlook when talking to their clients, yet it effectively sets the stage for the rest of the estate planning documents. This is something that you, not your attorney, create that explains what you want your final years to look like.

---

7 Ibid.
8 Laura J. Martin, "Do-not-resuscitate Order," MedlinePlus: National Institutes of Health, https://medlineplus.gov/ency/patientinstructions/000473.htm.

In a letter of intent, you outline the kind of end-of-life care you want to receive, the financial extent someone should go to to provide that care, and when to transition from one level of care to another. Every other document in this chapter talks about what happens when you are incapacitated or dead, but none of them really lets your loved ones know how you want to live your remaining years. If you do not want to live with your children, or you want to be placed in a certain assisted living facility, this is where you can declare that information. Do not make your loved ones decide for you.

This document can also include the kind of funeral service you want to have, where it will be held, and whether you want your favorite '80s rock singer to sing at your funeral.

Life Is Short

Have you known someone, maybe even you, who had a life-altering experience that made something "click" in their consciousness, and they started doing things differently? In a profession like mine, you see a lot of interesting situations.

For example, there was one client who had a near-fatal heart attack, and it wasn't certain for a while whether he would pull through. Eventually, after some major surgery and grueling physical therapy, he emerged completely changed. While he had been a lifelong introvert, suddenly it was like a light had turned on inside him. He would talk to anyone and everyone. He picked up new hobbies and went on a spontaneous two-month jaunt to Asia and Australia. And he came to realize that the people most important to him had stayed by his side even though he had not been there for them as much. He vowed then to dedicate the rest of his life to spending time with the family that had stood by his bed.

Researchers Richard Tedeschi and Lawrence Calhoun call this type of response "post-traumatic growth."[9] It is a period of emotional development in which we become acutely aware of our mortality and realize the life we have been living isn't what we had envisioned.

My client was lucky, because he had this epiphany before it was too late. He also realized he wouldn't be around forever, and it was time to take estate planning seriously.

It doesn't matter what your background is, where you went to school, or how smart you think you are—death and disability are around every corner. While I choose not to live my life in fear of the unknown, I know how important it is to make sure you have the right documents in place, with the right people able to step in, so your life can continue around you with very little interruption in the event of a devastating emergency. The last thing you want is to have your child at college be injured and find yourself unable to make medical decisions on their behalf, or be a business owner whose firm cannot make payroll because you didn't have the right legal tools in place to reduce disruption.

It doesn't matter if you are a business owner, a soccer mom, or a student—*everyone* needs some combination of these documents at different stages in life. Make sure you review you documents annually to remember who is doing what, whether they are still able to step into their role if you cannot, and whether certain changes need to be made if your life has significantly changed.

---

9 Jim Rendon, "How Trauma Can Change You—for the Better," *Time,* July 22, 2015, http://time.com/3967885/how-trauma-can-change-you-for-the-better/.

T I P

The right combination of estate planning documents, with the correct integration of financial planning, can save families stress, frustration, and money. I have read many estate documents drafted with the best intentions that did not appropriately integrate the family's financial planning objectives. For example, failing to integrate clauses that protected against "creditors, predators, in-laws and outlaws" created legacy issues for future generations. If protecting your family and assets during your life was important, why wouldn't you want to protect your wealth and your heirs from outsiders after you're gone? This can protect hundreds of thousands of dollars, if not millions, when your heirs inherit your fortune.

CHAPTER 10

A Blueprint That Endures for Years

Holy crap! You did it! You stuck around and made it through the meat of the book. That's no small feat. Financial planning is tough, even if you have an advisor to guide you (though that also means you have to sit in my office and listen to me delve into the complexities of taxation, investment, and so on for two to four hours). But it's even more challenging if you're guiding and teaching yourself with this book as your toolbox.

I would love to tell you that now the work is completed and you can tuck everything you have done away for the next couple of years and go about your life. But remember the analogy from before about buying a car and not taking it in for an oil change or tune-up? You have to stay on top of the plan if you want to make sure you are successful.

Financial planning is like going to the doctor for your annual physical, except without the awkward probing and paper-thin backless hospital gown. Sure, you are going to get deep. The topics are going to get intense, maybe even uncomfortable. You might have to turn your head and cough while a CFP® checks under the hood—financially speaking, of course. I'm not that kind of advisor.

No one likes visiting the doctor, but it's a necessary chore that leaves you better when you walk out than when you came in: spotlighting risks, rectifying problems, easing fears, and bringing you closer to a long, healthy, joyful life.

And just like visiting the doctor, the work is not done once you leave the clinic. You need to practice healthy habits and make adjustments as life goes on. Financially, that means you need to stay on top of the changes in your life, on top of the changes in the market, and on top of what the government is doing.

It might sound like a lot, but it doesn't have to be. If you do it periodically over the course of the year, it'll be manageable.

The first step involved in the systematic review is deciding whether you want to take the "doing" or "delegating" approach.

The "Doer Mentality"

In chapter 4 we talked about the differences between taking on tasks yourself and outsourcing them to others. Some of the most successful people in the world *delegate* what they do not have the time and/or skill for and *do* what they do have the time and/or skill for.

For the doers of the world, here are the three steps you need to take throughout the year and at the end of every year in order to make sure your ship doesn't sink before reaching its final destination: the Ongoing Review, the Check-In, and the Annual Check-Up.

Step One: The Ongoing Review

Unfortunately, "ongoing review" doesn't just mean "once in a while." In fact, I strongly encourage clients to review their finances weekly. Yes, weekly. For fifteen to twenty minutes a week, on a Saturday or Sunday, over a cup of coffee, tea, or other pleasurable beverage, you need to update and categorize your bills in your budget/ cash flow statement. This gives you a clear picture of your current spending and how much money you have remaining in each category of your budget.

If a weekly examination doesn't sound reasonable, the alternative is to conduct the review once a month, although this is not ideal, since it turns a breezy fifteen- to twenty-minute per week task into an hour or longer chore. It's best to break down the tedium of reconciling your finances into small, manageable chunks. Otherwise, it becomes more frustrating and painful, and what is supposed to be done at the end of the month turns into an every other month, or once a quarter, occurrence. After a long-enough period, the three-to-four hour task each quarter becomes overwhelming, and most people will just stop doing it altogether.

You're a doer, right? So "do!" Follow through on the plan you originally laid out by taking the quarter hour per week to check in. Everyone can find fifteen minutes to spare. You probably spend more time each week thinking about what you are going to have for dinner.

In addition to weekend reviews, you will also need to spend two or three hours once a quarter reviewing your investments. This does not mean you need to do an overhaul of the portfolio, but you need to make sure the reason you first invested in those securities is still valid based on the economic and political environment at that time. Many investors elect to follow passive investing strategies over active strategies because active strategies often underperform their benchmark. As I pointed out in chapter 7, on average, actively managed funds exceed their comparable benchmark only 40 percent to 50 percent of the time over a one-year period, a success rate that declines steeply on longer timelines.[1] If your portfolio needs updating, then you may need to invest additional time researching new investment options.

This means that if you stay on top of your portfolio, you can make the necessary adjustments throughout the year to concentrate on the best-performing investments. However, if you would prefer to stay hands off, passive investing is probably best. This essentially concentrates your money in reliable market-mirrored investments (like index funds) where trying to outperform the market is an afterthought at best. I liken passive investing to riding a rollercoaster: If you like being a passenger on a rollercoaster without much in the way of guard rails, then index investing might be perfect for you.

Step Two: The Check-In

After you have completed your weekly audits and your first quarterly review of your portfolio, you will need to conduct a check-in review at the six-month mark. This means you need to spend thirty to ninety minutes, on top of the second quarter investment review, reviewing your spending habits over the first six months. This gives you a more comprehensive, big-picture look at your budget to supplement the weekly review.

If you spent less in the first six months than your budget allowed for, then are you doing with the surplus cash flow? Conversely, if you overspent, why did you? Was this an anomaly, or is it a trend that deserves a closer look? Maybe you need to either cut back or increase your budget over the next six-month period.

---

1 Aye M. Soe and Ryan Poirier, "SPIVA U.S. Scorecard," 2016, https://us.spindices.com/documents/spiva/spiva-us-year-end-2016.pdf.

It should be said that when you elect to increase your budget, you need to also adjust other areas of your cash flow, like your savings goals. This prevents you from overspending and making unnecessary withdrawals from your emergency fund. Remember, the emergency fund is there in case your car breaks down, your roof is damaged, or your child gets sick. The emergency fund is designed to help bail you out, not act as a slush fund.

Once the check-in is complete, you can begin adjusting your foundational documents. You will be able to validate your cash flow statement, see the impact on your balance sheet, and check off which goals you have met. A good example of why reconciling these statements is beneficial is if you see your cash flow statement break even but your balance sheet goes down. I have seen situations where clients think their budget is on track, but their checking, savings, or emergency fund accounts are lower than they were at the beginning of the year. In such situations, I have to conduct some forensic accounting to see if there is an error in the math or if they actually spent more than they thought. Remember, garbage in equals garbage out.

Step Three: The Annual Check-Up

By now, you are a pro at the process. You already have the weekly audits down, you conduct your quarterly investment reviews, and you have performed your six-month check-in. At the Annual Check-Up point, there are only three tasks you need to perform. The first is to repeat what you did at the six-month check-in. The second is to review your goals and determine if you need to remove or add goals to the list. This will help you stay on track, adjust the plan based on significant events and life changes, and allow you to acknowledge your accomplishments over the prior year. The third is to re-review your insurance coverages as discussed in chapter 6, compare your investment return to your target personal return, revisit your tax plan, and confirm that your estate plan is still valid. Then make changes as needed to each section.

Finally, taking a moment to acknowledge your recent achievements is hugely important. In fact, without a little bit of well-deserved celebration, the whole process will seem more like a "job" rather than a pleasurable experience (at least as pleasurable as personal finance can be).

Then, when you are done with the annual review, you simply rinse and repeat the process every year, checking off your goals as you accomplish them.

The "Delegator Mentality"

If the thought of adding all these extra tasks to your already jammed schedule makes your head spin, I understand. Most of the individuals who hire my company's services are completely capable of managing their finances but are too busy to do so, so they decide to delegate the tasks they do not have an interest in or that they prefer not to conduct on their own. They have decided their time is better spent on other areas of their lives and choose to hire a trusted advis*or* or advis*er* to handle it, freeing up time to spend doing what they want.

The advisor/adviser–client relationship, like all relationships, is based on trust. But it can be hard to gauge someone's trustworthiness, especially in the first meeting, before you get to know them.

So how do you know whom you can count on? And what exactly should you look for in an advisor/adviser? For the answer to that question, I developed a questionnaire you can use to help locate someone who gels with you, your goals, and your thought process. Don't just pick someone because they seem like a "good person" or because of their intelligence. Those attributes are good, but more importantly, you need to feel a connection with them. That connection is what will forge the trust on which your professional relationship will thrive. Remember, this person is going to hear stories about some of your most intimate struggles. Some of my clients regard me almost like a member of their own family. In some cases, they divulge more about their finances to me than they do to even their closest kin.

To find someone you can trust, consider the following questions to ask, in no particular order:

1. What securities and/or insurance licenses do you have? (i.e., Series 7, Series 6, Series 65, Series 63, Series 66, etc.)

2. What are your credentials—your certifications or designations? (i.e., CFP®, ChFC®, CFA®, CPA, EA)

3. Are you a fiduciary for my nonqualified *and* qualified accounts? What qualifies you to be one? *(This will help you determine whether they are required to put your interests ahead of their own.)*

4. How long have you personally been in the financial services business?

5. What made you decide to stay in the business?

6. What happens to our relationship, or my accounts, if you are no longer here? *(Will you just be passed off to someone else who doesn't know you or are you allowed to interview a replacement?)*

7. What is the turnover rate in your office? *(If people leave often, there could be problems within the company.)*

8. Will you still be in the industry when I am in my eighties? *(This addresses the relationship's prospect for longevity.)*

9. How do you charge for your services (i.e., fee only, fee-based, or commission)?

10. If you are paid a commission, will you divulge how much you will be paid for placing my business? *(Remember, if they are going to receive a one-time check of $2,000 or $20,000 for placing business on your behalf as opposed to an ongoing compensation, then you need to make sure you understand what you are investing in, because their level of support may trail off if they are not compensated after the initial sign-up.)*

11. Do I have to invest my assets with you in order for you to help me? If so, what is the minimum?

12. What is your investment philosophy? *(If they believe in a long-term "buy and hold" strategy, they are likely to only make minor, periodic changes to your investments. If most funds underperform their comparable indexes over the long run, this could negatively affect you. Being more proactive in the strategy can offer you an opportunity to find investments that outperform their investment benchmarks, though this is not guaranteed. Past performance is no guarantee of future results.)*

13. How often can we meet? How accessible are you?

14. How many clients do you actively work with on a regular basis? *(This will give you an idea about whether you will be a name or merely a number amongst a large pool of other clients.)*

After speaking with your prospective advisor/adviser, ask yourself the following questions:

1. Did the advis*or* or advis*er* actively listen to you and your needs during the meeting?

2. Did you feel the advis*or* was pushing a particular product or service on you?

3. Did you feel comfortable with the person or company you spoke with?

4. Did they seem to avoid making eye contact with you? Were their arms crossed throughout the meeting? *(That kind of body language sometimes signals a lack of interest.)*

5. Were they upfront about any potential conflicts of interest? Do they work on your behalf or that of the company that employs them? *(This can help you assess their motivation for recommending certain products or services.)*

6. Can you see yourself working with this person for many years?

7. Did you feel like a person or a number in the meeting?

These questions will help you examine how the advisor's answers align with your personal feelings and needs. Remember, if you are going to open up to someone about something as important as your finances, you need to feel you can fully trust them. Your future is in their hands.

Bringing It All Together

Now you have the necessary knowledge to build a sound financial plan. Just like a blueprint for a house, this knowledge, if used correctly, will allow you to bring your dreams to life. Over time, you will integrate that blueprint with your own unique vision of the details of your house—such as what kind of paint to put on the walls or which furniture you should buy and where it should go. As you maintain the upkeep on your financial house, some of the pieces of your plan will change over time along with your personality and goals.

Finally, deciding when to be a doer and when to be a delegator may be the factor that determines your future success. If you have the skill, will, and time to tackle the tasks outlined in this book, I encourage you to do it yourself. But make sure you have a backup plan in case you lose interest, become incapacitated, or your significant other is forced to take over in your absence. And if you choose to delegate, make sure to choose the right person. Whatever path you take, keep your head down, stay on task, and do not be afraid to ask for help when you need it—not when it's twenty years too late.

Throughout my career helping people with their finances, I've gotten to intimately know people's hopes, fears, passions, and what makes them tick. I like to say that I've lived a thousand lifetimes in one. Each client's story is different, but there are certain strategies and actions that can empower everyone regardless of their age, wealth, income, or family status. And I'm not just "talking the talk"; I use these same strategies to protect my own family.

It's true that sometimes life can be dismal, dangerous, and checkered by risk. In the hardest moments, it can feel like your well-being is threatened at every turn. But life can also be beautiful, joyous, carefree, and secure. It's up to you to build the life you want. And now you have the master plan. It won't always be easy, but embrace the challenge. I know you can do it.

BONUS

CHAPTER 11

Divorce and Finances

I'll never forget the day I heard the words "I want a divorce." It was eleven o'clock at night and we had just had a bitter fight. When those devastating words left her mouth, my heart sank and I felt sick to my stomach. My pulse raced and adrenaline shot through me as I wracked my brain, trying desperately to think of some way to salvage my marriage.

It's in my nature to try to solve problems. It's what I do for a living—a fixer of crises by trade. Yet at that moment, I was completely ignoring the feelings of discontentment I, too, had long had. Later, I learned that neither of us had been happy in our marriage, and we had both been looking for the right time to tell the other. She just had the intestinal fortitude to say it before me.

While the divorce was hard for both of us, we cared deeply for each other and didn't want to hurt each other. As a matter of fact, before we were married, we had been friends for many years, and our affectionate "us versus the world" mentality had always been the basis of our close bond.

Then, when we got married, we quickly realized how different we were in some of the most important ways (i.e., child-rearing, finances, roles), but we did our best to make the circumstances work. In fact, after a short while, she became my role model for multi-tasking: I was blown away by the number of things she could juggle in a single day. This, of course, led to many arguments over the years about why I couldn't do what she could, to which I would say that I just didn't have her superhuman abilities.

When the time came for us to sit down and start dividing assets, we both agreed we didn't want to involve attorneys. Both she and I had been screwed over by the legal system in the past, so we sat down, cranked out the numbers ourselves, and drafted the necessary papers on our own. We even went down to the courthouse and filed the paperwork together. Handling the divorce pro se—when two parties file on their own, without professional legal help—was probably the best thing we could have done. It allowed us to work through a lot of "our" issues together, almost like therapy, and allowed us to end the marriage as friends instead of adversaries. This was hugely beneficial as it helped us improve our communication about our children and other issues. We actually became better friends divorced than when we were married.

Now, I do not necessarily advocate a pro se divorce over hiring an attorney. Rather, I urge couples to take the approach that is best for them, their pocketbooks, and their kids. In many cases, attorneys offer help when other solutions are not viable. But if attorneys *are* involved, I advocate for clients to take an active role in the process in order to maintain a level of control *and* to ideally reduce the legal expenses.

While divorce can be a hefty expense, it's the emotional toll that really hurts. I am sure we can all agree divorce is a wrenching process. As emotions run high, it is common to look for the quickest way out. Nevertheless, if you are considering divorce, it is important to educate yourself on the financial impact and learn to separate your emotions from your finances during the weeks, if not months, leading up to asking for a divorce. As you begin mentally preparing yourself for the unknown, I encourage you to also prepare financially using these five steps.

1. The Budget, Balance Sheet, and Goal Statement Before and After Divorce

Barring a stock market crash or a debilitating health crisis, few events impact your finances as dramatically as a divorce. You can lose half the assets you've spent a lifetime accumulating, and recovering financially can be a huge undertaking. In the face of all this upheaval, you should revisit the worksheets we discussed in chapter 3 and evaluate the impact of divorce on your financial situation. That means those three key documents: the budget, balance sheet, and goal statement.

A *budget* (aka cash flow statement) is the linchpin for evaluating and planning for the future. However, budgets are only as good as the information they hold. This document, which lays out your gross and net income along with an itemized list, by category, of your expenses, allows you to re-prioritize, when necessary, your spending habits after the household income changes. It is vital to understand where the "household" money is spent today and which of those expenses will carry forward after divorce. Additionally, try to think about what new ongoing expenses you will need to pay. Both during separation and after divorce, mapping out where your money goes today and what will change in the future will help you in your settlement negotiations.

A *Balance Sheet* is a comparison of assets and liabilities. If you have ever taken inventory of what you own and how much you owe, you are more than halfway done. This tool lays out what resources can be used to help reach your immediate and future financial goals. This document will be used to determine which assets are owned by each spouse, which assets make more sense to fight for, and whether someone is hiding anything. Once you know what you have, you can allocate resources to your short-term goals.

A *Goal Statement* is a detailed list of current and future goals along with any associated expenses. If some of the goals are expected to continue after the divorce, you can assess their probability of completion with the available cash flow and assets. When "mutual interest goals" like paying for a child's college exist, this document can be used to negotiate who will be paying for those goals and what the respective party's contribution will be. Harvard may no longer be a reality for little Jimmy, so both of you will need to come up with Plan B.

2. Living Arrangements Before and After Divorce

Determining where you will live after divorce is just as important as managing your finances. The primary residence be a sticking point in the settlement negotiations. In many cases, both spouses fight over their primary residence without understanding the financial impact on either spouse of keeping the home.

If you end up keeping the home, you need to determine very quickly how that expense will impact your cash flow and what other current, or future, goals it may take away from. Remember the debt-to-income ratio outlined in chapter 5: if the outflow consumes more than 35 percent of your gross monthly cash flow, consider other living options, as the cost of servicing that debt and ongoing maintenance will gradually increase. If your income doesn't keep up, you could put yourself in a very bad place.

3. *Divorce Can Change Your Marginal Tax Bracket*

Remember to consider taxes in your settlement options *and* consider what marginal income tax bracket you are in before and after divorce. In chapter 8, we talked about marginal and effective tax rates and walked through how decisions made today can have dire ramifications years down the line. Unfortunately, an event like a divorce can have an immediate effect on both spouses' taxes in the year of the divorce *and* for the first few years after the divorce.

In 2018, a married couple making an adjusted gross income of $77,000 will be in the 12 percent marginal bracket, whereas a single filer with an adjusted gross income of $77,000 will be in the 22 percent marginal bracket. As you negotiate who will be the custodial parent, which assets you split, and which assets are ultimately liquidated, consider how taxes could affect your net (after-tax) cash flow. Furthermore, alimony will need to be taken into account, as it can dramatically impact the tax situation of the payer, since from January 1, 2019, alimony is no longer deductible under the Tax Cuts and Jobs Act of 2017.

4. *Child Support versus Spousal Support*

When considering divorce, it is important to understand all cash flow options, or obligations. For those with children, child support is determined at the state level and calculated based on a predetermined formula from the state. Spousal support, on the other hand, is typically negotiable between spouses, with the final decision in the hands of the presiding judge. If you expect to pay or receive one or both of these support payments, it is important to consider how long the income will last. This information will factor into your standard of living, housing arrangements, and your expected budget after divorce.

5. Maintaining Employer Benefits

Health insurance, flexible spending accounts, life insurance, and retirement savings are just a few examples of resources that may be in jeopardy during divorce negotiations. If getting divorced means you will lose access to any of these benefits, you will need to evaluate the costs of acquiring them all over again. As an example, if you need to acquire health insurance for you or for your children, make sure you include that expense in your monthly obligations and assess the impact on net cash flow. The law today allows the divorcee to carry the other spouse's insurance via COBRA, if insured prior to divorce, for up to thirty-six months. However, COBRA can be quite expensive. If there are children, it would be wise to discuss keeping them on the insurance plan under the primary insurance holder. This reduces the total cost out of pocket for insurance and keeps them insured past thirty-six months.

Divorce Team

Before you become too involved in divorce proceedings, it is important to assemble a quality divorce team. No, I don't mean your two college drinking buddies you haven't seen in five years; your wild, perpetually single friend; and the hair stylist you gossip with once a month. (I know I am guilty of this.)

The divorce team I'm talking about is comprised of professionals who see to your legal, financial, and emotional needs. The initial members of your team will be your divorce attorney, their legal support staff, and maybe a therapist, when appropriate. In the same way that a musician in an orchestra has an individual role that contributes to a larger ensemble, so do the members of your divorce team.

For more complex cases, or for those involving liquid assets in excess of roughly $250,000, the team may expand to include other attorneys, accountants, a mediator or arbitrator, and other professionals deemed appropriate by you and your attorney.

Usually, your divorce attorney will take the lead and interact with your ex-spouse and/or their attorney on your behalf. The other members of the team will play a supporting role and work with you and your attorney to provide relevant information pertaining to your case.

However, there is one member of this team who will eventually become critical in helping you and your attorney evaluate different divorce financial solutions. That member is the Certified Divorce Financial Analyst® (CDFA®), aka the divorce financial planner. According to the Institute of Divorce Financial Analysts, the role of the CDFA® is to assist the client and his/her lawyer in understanding how the financial decisions the client makes today will impact the client's financial future.

Now some people might ask, "Well, isn't my attorney versed in financial matters?" To be fair, some attorneys have accumulated a fair amount of financial expertise throughout their legal careers, but that doesn't mean they understand all of the complicated ins and outs and the myriad financial challenges you are about to face. Additionally, if the divorce proceedings hit a few bumps and a financial expert is needed to provide third party testimony, the attorney cannot fulfill that role—but a CDFA® can.

A CDFA® goes through intensive training on topics like these:

1. Completing detailed financial projections for different settlement options

2. How the nuances of spousal support versus child support can affect your tax situation

3. The impact of dividing current assets and guaranteed income on your retirement

4. Evaluating the cash flow impact of taking over the primary residence and how it affects saving for other goals

5. Forecasting your insurance needs to protect your standard of living, replace lost alimony payments, guard against a premature disability or death, and more

6. How to evaluate, develop, and manage a budget after divorce

7. Determining the appropriate investment risk of your portfolio for your short and long-term goals, after divorce

It should be said that while a CDFA® can offer a lot of financial guidance to you and your attorney, they do not provide legal advice. Their job is to act in a support role, leaving all court-related activity to your attorney.

Divorce Financial Solutions

Financial planning during and after a divorce should be approached from the perspective of "starting over." For example, completing a retirement analysis for a divorcee needs to reflect potential irregular cash flow from alimony and child support—"irregular" because in some cases, it is not paid consistently, or in perpetuity. Additionally, now that everything in your life has been upended, the necessary savings rates and required rate of return needed to reach future goals might change. This analysis can help to outline an appropriate risk level in accord with your goals (which may themselves also change).

There are plenty of advisors out there who can state that they work with divorced clients. However, before employing their services, you should inquire whether they practice "divorce financial planning" or financial planning for people who have been divorced. The former showcases they work with *divorcing* or *recently divorced* individuals, while the latter highlights working with someone who may have been divorced at one point in their life. Depending on how far removed from a divorce someone is, they may or may not share the concerns noted above. Be sure to ask this when looking for an advisor.

Other Financial Considerations

Needless to say, each divorce case is unique; there is no one-size-fits-all approach. Make sure the people working for you address all the concerns particular to your case and your concerns.

You and your attorney or advisor should include the following in your financial discussions:

1. What state statutes govern the divorce process (i.e., community property or common law state)?

2. Based on your experience, how are financial and personal use assets divided in this state? Can an argument be made by one spouse that they are entitled to receive more of the marital assets (e.g., an upfront alimony buyout, a settlement note, a larger portion of marital assets being allocated to one spouse than to the other due to the amount of separate property each spouse already owns)?

3. If alimony will be paid to one spouse, how is it calculated? If it is negotiated into the divorce decree, how long can someone expect it be paid?

4. If children are involved, who will have primary physical custody and how will child support be calculated?

5. How should a pension of future payments be calculated, valued, and divided in a divorce?

6. Should a "property settlement note" be used to divide an illiquid asset, like a closely held business or an alternative investment?

7. Who will take care of drafting and executing a Qualified Domestic Relations Order (QDRO)? A QDRO is a judicial order governing how an employer retirement or pension plan is divvied up between divorcing spouses. Will it be done before the divorce is finalized?

Each of the above questions comes with a myriad of possible financial solutions. In order to select the best solution, the CDFA® on your divorce team will begin by compiling and assessing your entire financial life into a set of documents (i.e., cash flow statement, balance sheet, goal statement, insurance assessment, and much more). They'll consider the impact of a property settlement agreement and other matters. Then the final assessment will provide an impact analysis that can be used by your attorney to address the questions listed above and many others.

Let's discuss some examples of how the above questions can impact your life after divorce.

Community Property versus Common Law

Each state has a set of statues that govern how all assets will be titled—that is, who officially owns these assets. This titling of ownership will later govern how those assets will be divided in the case of divorce or death. According to FindLaw.com, "The common law system provides that property acquired by one member of a married couple is owned completely and solely by that person. Of course, if the title or deed to a piece of property is put in the names of both spouses, however, then that property would belong to both spouses. If both spouses' names are on the title, each owns a one-half interest." [1]

Alternatively, "the states having community property are Louisiana, Arizona, California, Texas, Washington, Idaho, Nevada, New Mexico, and Wisconsin. Community property states follow the rule that all assets acquired during the marriage are considered 'community property.' Marital property in community property states are owned by both spouses equally (50/50). This marital property includes earnings, all property bought with those earnings, and all debts, accrued during the marriage." [2]

It should be noted that in some states gifts given to one person, and not both spouses, can be considered separate property.

Now that you have a basic understanding of how different states classify marital property, you can work with your attorney to come up with an equitable distribution. A quality divorce attorney can work within the confines of the law to come up with a fair plan that serves you best.

Furthermore, after a CDFA® has conducted their assessment of the household assets, the attorney can work with their client to determine which assets are the highest priority. In other words, if one spouse wants the house with a lot of equity, then the CDFA® can determine which of the other assets offer a comparable substitution for that lost equity. The last thing anyone wants is to be stuck with a larger tax bill or an unplanned inequitable distribution after the divorce is finalized.

1 "Who Owns What In Marital Property?" FindLaw, family.findlaw.com/marriage/what-s-mine-is-mine-what-s-yours-is-mine-who-owns-what-in.html.
2 Ibid.

Alimony

Alimony is the financial support one spouse must pay to the other as part of a court-ordered divorce settlement. Interpreted differently by each state, alimony can be classified as "bridge the gap," "rehabilitative," or "permanent." For example, Florida determines which type of alimony is eligible for payment based on the number of years the couple is married.[3] Other states take a different approach.

Over the last couple of decades, there has been a shift away from mandatory support obligations to determining qualifications for support, based on the presumption that both spouses have worked or are able to work and thus negating the argument for permanent alimony. However, there are circumstances in which transitional alimony (bridge the gap or rehabilitative) is justified, but those circumstances are usually based in immediate financial needs. As with any important legal matter, seek the counsel of your attorney to figure out your particular situation.

In the event that you expect to pay alimony, it is possible to negotiate that the payments be made for a specific period of time. This can allow the receiving party to maintain a certain standard of living while transitioning back into society. Alternatively, the payment time period can be linked to predetermined adjustments in the financial well-being of the receiving spouse. For example, if the receiving spouse's income exceeds a certain level or if the receiving spouse cohabitats with another person, then the alimony payments would stop.

It is important to note that under the Tax Cut and Jobs Act of 2017, the tax adjustment for alimony payments between two spouses

---

3 "Alimony," Title VI, 61.08, 2017 Florida Statutes, http://www.leg.state.fl.us/Statutes/index.cfm?App_mode=Display_Statute&URL=0000-0099/0061/Sections/0061.08.html.

ends on December 31, 2018. Therefore, anyone who is divorced, or in the process of divorce, before that date will be grandfathered in under the old rules. Those filing for divorce after December 31, 2018, and expecting to pay alimony will shoulder the full tax responsibility of the alimony payments. It will be interesting to see if divorce attorneys will fight for the payments to be lower since the paying spouse will be responsible for the full tax burden of paying alimony.

Illiquid Assets

Another concern of divorcing couples relates to illiquid assets. When it comes to real estate investments, private placements, or ownership of a small business, there may be few options for liquidation. Therefore, an alternative solution is needed to properly divide these kinds of assets. In these situations, a "property settlement note" can be used by one spouse to buy out, or pay off, the other spouse's share in the illiquid asset. Additionally, this note can be assigned a market interest rate if paid out over a period of time and collateralized if there is a concern about payback.

There are some caveats, though, to using a property settlement note. The first is to make sure the person initiating the buyout, or payback, can maintain the ability to make installment payments. The second deals with the asset itself. One spouse maintains ownership of the asset and is able to benefit from the asset's growth in value over time, while the other spouse is paid their portion over a period of time, instead of in a lump sum. Therefore, the spouse receiving the payment needs to make sure the determined market rate reasonably reflects the growth of the illiquid investment, or that of a comparable investment.

Lastly, when I counsel a client and their attorney during the negotiation process, I encourage them to instruct the person paying the settlement note to obtain additional life insurance. This way the recipient has a higher probability of receiving their full payout. To provide an incentive to the payer, the payments of life insurance can be negotiated in the calculation of alimony, therefore reducing how much is required to be directly paid to the other spouse.

Pensions

As we discussed earlier, each state's laws determine which assets and income are included in the marital estate. This may mean that a portion (if not all) of a spouse's pension may be included in the marital estate. The same concern for illiquidity mentioned above applies to pensions; however, there are a few points every divorced person should be aware of before negotiating for the pension.

1. A private or government-sponsored pension is essentially a promissory note by an organization to pay a stream of income for a period of time. Underfunded private pensions are at risk of failing to deliver promised benefits.

2. The promissory note is usually calculated based on three factors: how long an individual has worked for the organization, their highest three salary years, and an assumed growth rate.

3. The pension payment is usually contingent on the employee remaining with the organization until payment date to maintain full eligibility. If an employee terminates employment early, their pension payment could be reduced or eliminated, which means so will your payment.

4. Unless backed by the full faith and credit of the US government, pension payments are not necessarily guaranteed. In cases of bankruptcy, pensions can be reduced or even lost depending on a variety of factors. Examples like Enron, MCI WorldCom, and

General Motors remind everyone how pension benefits can go up in smoke if the company fails. Of course, most pensions are protected by the Pension Benefit Guaranty Corporation, but even they do not guarantee pension payments to 100 percent, only to a fixed amount that changes periodically.

If a client decides they want to pursue their portion of their spouse's pension, it becomes very important for the CDFA® or a valuation expert to perform a "present value calculation," in which the analyst determines the present value of the future cash flow payments that will be paid at some point in the future. The result of this calculation can help the attorney and their client decide if a buyout of future income is worth the risk of waiting to collect funds at some date in the future. If the buyout is opted for, and agreed to by both parties, this becomes another means by which a larger percentage of marital assets today can be shifted from one spouse to another.

Child Support

Once upon a time, many mothers could count on being awarded custody of the minor children. However, now, depending on the state you reside in, the age of your children, and the location of both parents, many courts use alternative custody arrangements. Your divorce attorney can help you navigate the laws in your state concerning joint legal custody, primary physical custody, shared custody, visitation, and so on. This is another case where hiring a divorce financial planner can be useful. They're trained to handle these tricky issues. For example, if the parents are awarded joint legal custody with shared physical custody, a child support payment is not guaranteed.

If you are awarded a monthly support payment, be sure to find out how that payment is calculated. Many states offer online calculators[4] to help gauge the payment, though these calculators only provide estimates and are not legally binding.

Also, check with your attorney on whether or not health insurance and childcare costs are factored into the support calculation. Some states provide a "credit" toward the obligation to the parent providing health insurance, and some states separate childcare costs and bill them independently.

As with a potential spousal support payment, be careful when factoring child support into your monthly cash flow. While many states impose stiff penalties on noncompliant parents, it can take a long time before legal action compels the delinquent parent or their salary is garnished.

Divorcing with a Special Needs Child

Divorce is a scary endeavor in the best of circumstances, but divorcing with a special needs child involves an entirely different level of emotion and conflict. All children are impacted in one way or another by the nuclear family's dissolution. A nondisabled child might come to understand the "why" behind a divorce, but some special needs children have a harder time processing, accepting, and adapting to change. Inevitably, these children will need more support and a potentially longer transition period. In some cases, special needs children may require resources beyond those the immediate family can provide.

Family Transitions

From the moment you said "I do" to the birth of your first child, you probably felt you would be able to handle anything life threw

---

4 "Calculate Child Support Payments in Virginia," AllLaw.com, www.alllaw.com/calculators/childsupport/virginia.

your way. But when it comes to raising children, this confidence is regularly put to the test. Parents often think that their new bundle of joy is exceptional in many ways. But some parents may find that their child is growing and developing differently than other children their age. Children born with developmental delays, physical or emotional impairments, or other learning disabilities may not understand the obstacles that lay ahead of them. Therefore, it becomes the parents' responsibility to determine which, if any, changes the family should make to protect the child. These changes can include the following:

- One parent may quit their full-time job to take care of their child.
- The parents may seek additional support services to help the child adjust and adapt to their surroundings.
- The parents may consider how to employ community services for transportation or education and vocational help at school or work.

In the case of a divorce, these changes are potentially compounded. For example, the child may need additional transition support from therapists, care managers, advocates, and their close family network in order to cope with and process a divorce. It is imperative to completely understand the additional support services a child will need as the settlement agreement is being negotiated.

Financial Impact of Divorce

When a couple decides to divorce, the decision to split assets becomes less about two people and more about the couple and their special needs child or children. Consider these questions as you discuss dividing assets with your CDFA® and divorce attorney:

- What was the financial impact on the family of having one person stop their career to attend to their child's daily needs? What would it cost to reeducate that spouse to enter the workforce?
- Who will attend to the child's needs if both parents have to work now? What additional support services will be needed and who will pay for them?
- If your child will not be able to financially take care of themselves after they turn eighteen, how long should alimony and child support obligations continue to be paid to take care of him or her?

These questions do not even begin to adequately assess or address the needs of you or your child. It is important to speak with professionals like the ones mentioned in this chapter who are well versed in the financial impacts of divorce, and how divorce affects families with special needs children.

Life with a Special Needs Child after Divorce

In chapter 9, we talked a lot about the importance of estate planning. Divorcing couples need to evaluate and create a plan for their special needs child in the event that one parent becomes incapacitated or dies.

Before the divorce is finalized, both parents should conduct their own financial planning to assess their financial situation alone *and* in the event the other spouse suffers a premature death or disability. Only after this analysis is conducted can both parents evaluate the financial impact of divorce as it pertains to their special needs child. For example, if either parent is underinsured and suffers a tragic event, alimony and child support could be at significant risk. Furthermore, if either parent loses the ability to provide for themselves and their dependent child, this could severely jeopardize that child's well-being. This is why having appropriate life and disability insurance coverage is especially critical for protecting the parents and the child/children.

The next chapter looks more closely at the financial considerations of raising a special needs child.

You Are Not Alone

Although going through divorce is a scary process, let me leave you with one last point of reflection. You don't have to be alone as you contend with this great financial and emotional upheaval in your life. There are many resources available to help get through this difficult transition. Additionally, taking an active, level-headed role in your divorce is the best approach for all parties involved. Trying to be more logical and less emotional doesn't just spare you a lot of unpleasant conversations with your (ex-)spouse; it can also help you avoid paying unnecessary attorney fees over trivial things (even when in the moment those trivial things seem gigantic). While divorce can be a messy, costly process, that doesn't mean you have to be at the mercy of your soon-to-be ex-spouse *or* at the mercy of the attorneys. You can take back control.

BONUS

CHAPTER 12

Special Needs Financial Planning

I was twenty-one and had no understanding of what it meant to raise a child, let alone a stepchild who would end up being an amazing, smart, kind, and caring child with a developmental delay. Her mother and I had been friends since high school. We had dated for a few months in college but with full lives ahead of ourselves, we decided to go our separate ways. Yet we continued to stay in contact and eventually found ourselves back in each other's lives—this time, we thought, for good.

From engagement to marriage, the five months flew by. Then, in one whirlwind month, we were married, bought a new house, moved in together for the first time, combined our finances, found out we were having a wedding day baby, and to top it all off, I became a stepfather to a sweet little six-year-old girl who at the time struggled with some processing delays. Needless to say, we had a lot going on in our family.

I spoke previously about my ex-wife's superpowers in her management of the house, her two jobs (both of which she wanted), and her personal life. But it was her attentiveness to the children—her bottomless affection, and her saintly patience—that spoke to the kind of parent she wanted to be . . . at least until the kids hit ten. . . . Just kidding.

It took me a few years to learn from her how to parent, and in particular, how to parent a child with special needs. But as our oldest grew and matured into a wonderful teenager and young woman, I came to find that the educational support system that was designed to protect her—the same system that the Individual with Disabilities Education Act (IDEA) was created to protect—consistently failed to give her the support she needed.

Year after year, I sat in Individualized Education Plan (IEP)[1] meetings wondering what the teachers were doing for her. Then, in one especially frustrating meeting, I suddenly realized in a moment of clarity that the teachers, while they were doing the best they could given that they were overstressed and understaffed, were for all intents and purposes just doing the minimum to pass her from one grade to the next.

At that moment, I decided something had to change, but first, I needed to teach myself the educational, legal, and financial impacts of raising a special needs child. It was a humbling process, since I ended up learning that there were a number of issues I, as a special needs parent, was failing on. I had not set up the correct estate plan. I had not built a transition plan from high school with her. I had not thought about how to fund a "retirement of three." Just to name a few.

---

1 IEPs are a fundamental part of special education in the US. Teachers and other educational professionals are required by federal law to create one for each special education student.

All of these issues, and many others, began to weigh on me. As I began tackling them, one by one, I realized I wasn't the only parent out there who needed help, which became the reason I eventually built an entire business model around helping families with special needs children.

This chapter was written to help you understand three key concerns I address with each special needs family I work with: how to build a special needs team, the importance of trust planning, and how retirement may not be the sun and beaches previously described by those timeshare salespeople.

Building Your "Special Needs Team"

Special needs planning can be an intense process that requires the coordination of multiple individuals who form a "special needs team" capable of addressing the child's financial, educational, medical, and therapeutic needs. To start, the team should include a professional associated with each of the following areas: legal counsel, financial guidance, and advocacy. Family, friends, and the special needs counselor at school also play a vital role on the team.

Planning for the future is always a challenge, but special needs financial planning tends to be more complex. The earlier you start, the better equipped you'll be to face the challenges and uncertainties the future will throw your way. It is therefore important that you seek appropriate counsel with someone who understands special needs planning, like a special needs advisor and a special needs attorney. These individuals can assist you in outlining the tools, resources, and strategies to protect your and your loved one.

A qualified **special needs financial advisor**, such as a Chartered Special Needs Consultant™ (ChSNC™), can help you plan for your financial future and that of your spouse or partner and your special needs child. They can help you project financial requirements and create a strategy to get where you need to be based on where you're starting.

Created by the American College of Financial Services, which trains and certifies financial professionals, "the ChSNC™ is the only credential on the market designed to provide special needs families with an advisor competent enough to address their unique concerns."[2] My experience caring for my daughter and dealing with the often frustrating public education system was what inspired me to obtain this certification, and it's been one of the best things I've ever done, both personally and professionally.

Adding a ChSNC™ to your team can help you navigate the difficult financial decisions that lay ahead of you. This person can be especially valuable if they work closely with your attorney to make sure documents are drafted with the right investment strategy in mind. They can also act as the special needs individual's advocate when family dynamics get complicated (as in the case of divorce, for example).

Advocacy Groups

You can think of advocacy groups as allies who provide auxiliary support to your team—the Churchill to your Roosevelt. These groups offer a plethora of knowledge and resources for special needs individuals and their families. One of the more prominent groups is The Arc, which has been helping confused families for more than sixty years. This group provides tools, training, and education on person-centered planning, housing options, grant programs, self-advocacy,

---

2 "About ChSNC," The American College of Financial Services, https://www.theamericancollege.edu/designations-degrees/ChSNC.

and much more.[3] One of its notable benefits is the "pooled income trust," which we'll discuss later in this chapter.

Legacy Planning

There's no way around it: Estate planning is morbid. No one likes to think about what happens to their effects, affairs, and life when/if they become incapacitated or die. Consequently, many people put it off, to their detriment. But even for the most flagrant procrastinators, life imposes a deadline on this task—in a very literal sense of the word.

"When I die, what legacy will I leave?" is a question we all ponder, but it's one that creates an inevitable quandary for those of us with special needs children. Parents who have been directly involved in helping a child throughout their life wonder who will fill their shoes when they are no longer there.

Further complicating the picture, special needs individuals may not be able to articulate with the same ease as others, which can impede efforts to explain their desires to others. This means those supporting special needs individuals should encourage the caregivers to work with an attorney who focuses in special needs planning, not someone who does estate planning in general. It's like going to the doctor: If you've had persistent chest pain for months, you probably aren't going to see a general practitioner. You'd want to visit a cardiologist.

As noted earlier, people with special needs may have insufficient assets to self-insure against high future, or ongoing, expenses and may need government support through programs like Social Security, Social Security Disability Insurance, and/or Medicaid. Additionally, attorneys who assist individuals and families who may have significant

---

3 The Arc: https://www.thearc.org

assets, or could inherit significant assets, need to understand how to protect those assets in order for the special-needs individual to benefit from the assets without losing their government assistance.

For the aforementioned reasons, I encourage anyone seeking legal guidance for special needs planning to interview a couple of attorneys and inquire about their legal practice, their background, and how involved they are in their special needs clients' lives. Remember, you are the client, and the best client is an *informed* client. Do not be intimidated by the attorney's expertise or air of prestige, or by what they say. In fact, be aware of what they might *not* be saying.

The Role of Special Needs Trusts in Financial Planning

Trust planning is a tedious process that can be grimly summed up as, "When you die, where do you want all your crap to go?" Unpleasant to think about, surely, but it's a fact of life that we all must face. And if you have a special needs child, you have to consider an even greater number of circumstances.

Now, if you've already completed all your estate planning with your attorney, you might be tempted to say, "I've done all this already," and skip to the next section. Well, attorneys can help with a lot, but what they cannot do is predict the future. In other words, what is valid at the time of signing your estate documents may no longer be valid months, weeks, or even days afterward. If you or a loved one becomes disabled, or is born disabled, and your documents do not account for this event, then that may be a real problem for that person in the future when you die. This is where a special needs trust can offer some relief.

There are three primary trusts: a **self-settled trust**, a **pooled income trust**, and a **supplemental needs trust**. Each of these trusts offers different advantages, such as asset protection for the beneficiary, limited to no reduction in government benefits, and ongoing financial support. For example, properly drafted self-settled and supplemental needs trusts can bypass the Medicaid look back rules that normally penalize people for gifting or transferring an asset to another person or entity within five years of needing financial support from Medicaid.[4]

Self-settled trusts are usually designed and funded by the parent or grandparent of the special needs individual under the age of sixty-five. However, in 2016, a rule was changed to allow a special needs individual to create and fund a self-settled trust on their own, without having to go to court, as was the case prior to the rule change.[5] Basically, this type of trust allows the owner to place any funds in their name into this special trust. Once the funds are in the trust, the independent trustee can use the trust funds to pay for items that supplement whatever government support, like Medicaid, that person receives. An independent trustee can be basically anyone but it is recommended that the person is an advocate for the beneficiary and ideally someone who understands how to manage a special needs plan. Doing it this way means the funds last longer because Medicaid picks up the majority of the pre-negotiated expenses during life. Then, at the special needs individual's death, Medicaid is allowed to recoup all of the money it paid during the person's life. Since Medicaid rates can be cheaper than private insurance rates, depending on the investment strategy used in the trust, there is a chance additional funds could be left over to pass on to future heirs.

---

4 "Using a Medicaid Special Needs Trust When You Have Too Many Assets to Qualify," Nolo.com, https://www.nolo.com/legal-encyclopedia/using-special-needs-trust-when-you-have-too-many-assets-medicaid.html.
5 Special Needs Trust Fairness Act (H.R. 670/S. 349), National Academy of Elder Law Attorneys, Inc., https://www.naela.org/NAELADocs/114th SNTFA Updated 1pger.pdf.

Supplemental needs trusts offer an added level of benefits but cannot be created by the special needs individual. This trust serves to provide the beneficiary with additional needs (i.e., books, vacations, entertainment) through a third-party trust. The independent trustee is responsible for making sure the beneficiary's needs are met. This trust *cannot* pay for "eats and sheets," or food and shelter; if it does, the beneficiary is at risk of losing government benefits.

These trusts are usually created by close relatives, either outright or through a provision in their revocable trust. When drafted correctly, these trusts provide supplemental support after government benefits are paid to the special needs individual. Unlike the self-settled trust, if there are any funds left over after the death of the special needs individual, those funds can be transferred on to other heirs (heirs of the creators of the trust *or* of the special needs individual) per the trust document.

It is important to note that in the case of both trusts, the independent trustee *must not* call into question the language of the special needs trust. In the event that the trustee were to provide support for items such as food and shelter, government benefits could be reduced or eliminated for a period of time. Therefore, it is critical that the trustee of these trusts completely understand all of the rules associated with administering these special needs trusts.

Finally, the **pooled income trust** is simply a tool used by nonprofit organizations to "pool" assets of multiple families whose individual assets may be too small to qualify for financial institutional management. As a point of reference, not endorsement, the Arc is one such organization that offers this service. Often, when a financial institution is named as the trustee of a trust for which the institution's fee is too large relative to the size of the whole portfolio, that institution may recuse itself and defer the family to a pooled income trust offered by nonprofits.

A significant advantage of a pooled income trust has to do with the benefits received by the special needs individual. In the event the person exhausts their contribution to the pooled trust, they may be eligible to continue receiving ongoing financial support, though that depends on the nonprofit and its funding and distribution rules.

While a pooled income trust can be helpful, I encourage you to explore all options available before ceding control of your assets to any institutional program. The mission, vision, and values of an organization can change over time. While today a given nonprofit organization is dedicated to helping those with intellectual disabilities, its direction and focus could change later on in a way that might not always be great for the special needs individual. Just be sure to look carefully at all your options before committing to one.

Trusts and Tax Planning

Tax planning is another integral part of special needs financial planning. To that end, trusts help protect the financial assets of the special needs individual, including assets inherited by the individual from other members of the family. Assets held in these trusts are subject to the same, if not higher, tax rates that apply to individuals. However, depending on how trusts are integrated into a special needs plan, different trusts offer different benefits and create different consequences.

For example, consider someone who becomes disabled later in life. As the grantor, they can use an Intentionally Defective Grantor Trust (IDGT) to transfer property via a gift or sale. In return, the grantor receives a stream of income from the trust, presumably at a rate lower than the expected growth rate of the asset transferred, for a defined period of time. This income stream effectively qualifies as a "completed transfer" to an irrevocable trust, which removes it from being classified as an "available asset" for special needs planning purposes. If the asset is deemed an "available asset," then it is required to be exhausted before the individual would begin receiving government benefits. Removing it from their "available assets" means they can begin receiving government benefits right away. Any supplemental benefits would be paid for by the trust, preferably at Medicaid rates, which are typically less than prevailing rates.

While the beneficiary/grantor receives interest payments from the trust, those payments are not considered taxable income. Instead, during the payment period, any income generated in the IDGT is passed on to the beneficiary and taxed at their individual rate instead of at the trust's tax rate. Thus, if the primary investment strategy in the IDGT is appreciation instead of income, then any capital growth can be removed from their estate, and the income, if invested in tax-exempt, fixed-income securities, could potentially be tax-free. Of course, individual situations will vary and not everyone will qualify for this example. The point is, when building a sound estate plan, you need to look at special needs planning from multiple angles to make sure you are not negatively impacting another area.

Getting Into the Details: More Tax and Trust Scenarios

Part of the planning process requires understanding how taxes will affect financial resources in the future. Since tax planning is a very fluid process, it requires annual reassessments and revisions as needed. The following are just some examples of the tax considerations parents of a special needs child should think about.

1. They should determine whether their current special needs trust is set up as a "grantor" trust (i.e., an IDGT) or "non-grantor" trust (i.e., supplemental needs trust). If the trust is a grantor trust, then this is considered a "disregarded entity" by the IRS, and income from these trusts is taxed at the grantor's tax rates, on their 1040, which are usually more favorable than a non-grantor's trust tax rates. Alternatively, non-grantor trusts are deemed to be separate entities and as such are taxable as separate entities, which are typically in a higher tax bracket than an individual or grantor.

2. The tax structure of special needs trusts (SNT) versus that of Qualified Disability Trusts (QDT) can be very important. Understanding how a trust was established and who funded the trust will help determine who will ultimately be responsible for the taxable income generated in the trust. A qualified disability trust is allowed to take a much higher personal exemption ($4,150 in 2018) than the traditional simple and complex trusts ($100 and $300) discussed in chapter 9, thus lowering income taxes for the trust. These are the only personal exemptions that remained after Congress sliced up the tax code at the end of 2017. Many people, including inexperienced attorneys, are not familiar with how a special needs trust becomes a "qualified disability trust."[6,7]

3. Different trusts are allowed to be set up and funded from different parties (i.e., self-settled payback trusts, intentionally

---

6 "Qualified Disability Trusts Can Offer Tax Savings," Academy of Special Needs Planners, February 20, 2015, https://specialneedsanswers.com/qualified-disability-trusts-can-offer-tax-savings-12522.

7 http://www.wgcpas.com/news/alerts/887-tax-alert-agreement-on-tax-reform-impact-on-individuals.

defective grantor trusts, or third-party supplemental trusts). Determining whether the initial and consecutive contributions to the trusts are considered gifts, causing gift tax consequences, or taxable sales generating capital gains or interest income can be vital in determining who pays the taxable liability.

4. Think about the origin of the amount that will be used to initially fund the trust. For example, if it is a "grantor" trust and is being funded with the special needs individual's money, then it is not considered a completed transfer and, correspondingly, is not considered a gift—except in the case of a well-drafted IDGT, which is classified as a completed transfer. However, if you are funding a "non-grantor" trust for a special needs individual, then the amount you fund the trust with is considered a gift and could have gift tax consequences for you.

5. Needs-based government benefits, such as SSI (Supplemental Security Income) or Medicaid, can be impacted by unearned income (as defined by Social Security, rather than by the IRS) from special needs trusts distributions. The income generated from special needs trusts, if passed on directly to the beneficiary, can create a tax liability—without necessarily providing the cash needed to pay the corresponding tax bill. Additionally, as stated before, if income is passed on directly to the special needs individual, then it could trigger a reduction in government benefits.

There are still other tax strategies that special needs families should explore. For example, sometimes private tutoring by a specially trained teacher for therapeutic or behavioral support services may be classified as a valid medical expense (IRS Rev. Rule. 78.340). If considered a qualified expense (i.e., an expense related to private tutoring), then it might be eligible for a tax deduction. Additionally, those who qualify for impairment-related work expenses for attendant care services at their place of employment may be able to qualify for a business deduction in lieu of a medical deduction, which would avoid the Adjusted Gross Income (AGI) limitations of medical deductions (IRS Sections 67(d) and 190(b)(3)).

In order to make sure you are optimizing all of your eligible tax deductions, it is vital that you work with an enrolled agent or certified public accountant (or both) who is well versed in the needs of special needs families.

Retirement Planning

If you thought setting up the correct estate plan and managing your annual tax liability was hard, imagine planning for a life event that hasn't happened yet. But if there's anything this book has taught you, it's that thinking into the future is key.

Over the years, many of my clients have had the idea that retirement planning when you have a special needs child should be easy. They were under the assumption that nothing really changes from preretirement to postretirement. Yet there are some significant changes to prepare for, as in the following scenarios:

1. A disabled child with no work history was receiving SSI while their parents were working. This income was capped at $732 per month in 2017 and reduced under certain circumstances, like housing and food being provided to the individual.

2. Upon the start of a parent's Social Security benefits once the parent has retired, their child becomes eligible to switch to Social Security Disability Insurance under their retired parent's work history. In some cases, the benefit can be larger than

what they received under the SSI program and is not subject to the same restrictions outlined under SSI rules.

3. Upon Spouse A filing for Social Security retirement benefits, Spouse B, who never worked or didn't meet the required forty quarters for Social Security benefits, becomes eligible for a percentage of Social Security retirement benefits based on Spouse A's work history. How much they're eligible for is a product of two factors. The first is the actual filing date of spousal benefit. If Spouse B files before their full retirement age as specified by the Social Security Administration, then they will receive a reduced spousal benefit. The second factor is the pool of benefits available. In other words, when a spouse and a disabled child are both intending to access the retired individual's pooled family benefits, the pool is capped. This means anyone filing for any spousal benefits and dependent disability benefits might be competing for their fair share.

These three scenarios may not be universal or even common among special needs families, but they do point to an underlying concern. What benefits will the special needs child receive or lose at their parent's retirement?

Income Planning in Retirement

Many of my clients say they want to supplement their guaranteed income (i.e., pensions and Social Security) with the interest from their portfolio. Unfortunately, in a low interest rate environment, like the one we have experienced since 2007, they might not have that luxury. This means they are forced to live on either the principal or take on more risk to generate returns big enough to maintain their lifestyle without depleting their cash reserves.

For those who do not have guaranteed income sources, the pressure is even greater, since these people have to count on their portfolio income to pay for their expenses. Now add in the cost of caring for a spouse and/or an adult special needs child; their meticulously devised retirement income plan must now accommodate more than just themselves. This means they need to change their outlook on how to save, how much to save, and what kind of legacy they intend to leave that will be used to support their child when they no longer can.

Don't Be Intimidated

Although special needs financial planning can be extraordinarily complex, it need not be overwhelming, and it's nothing you can't handle. In fact, no doubt, you've already overcome much greater challenges. We're parents. Moving mountains is basically our life's work.

Delegators may take solace in the fact that there are resources out there to help and a whole cadre of niche professionals who dedicate their careers to solving the kinds of unique problems we've discussed in this chapter. Doers may find that their capacity for self-initiative is put to the test by these tasks, especially when it comes to the highly technical and often confusing interplay of disability law, finance, tax regulation, investment, and estate planning that constitute special needs financial planning. For example, devising an intentionally defective grantor trust, drafting the requisite documents, and then filing them in court is probably not something you're going to do on your own. Nevertheless, you can arm yourself with the information in this chapter when you work with attorneys and other professionals who *can* do all that for you. Knowledge—that's how you keep control of the situation and ensure that you're playing an active role in the process even if a specialist is handling the complicated grunt work for you.

Additional Resources

Resource #1:

    Jon Peyton

    www.jonpeyton.com

Resource #2:

    My Divorce Planner Podcast™

    www.mydivorceplan.com

Resource #3:

    The Entrepreneur's Adviser Podcast™

    www.entrepreneursadviser.com

Resource #4:

    Building An Exit Podcast™

    www.buildinganexit.com

Resource #5:

    Every Bit Special Podcast™

    www.everybitspecial.com

Financial Planning Provides No Guarantees

The results presented in this book are based on the historical information, personal experiences, readily available, and accessible, information. Any assumptions illustrated throughout the book are made in good faith. However, assumptions are by definition imprecise, and should not be construed as guarantees or projections. Moreover, the reasonableness of certain assumptions may change over time due to a variety of dynamic factors such as changes in your personal circumstances, in the economy, in tax laws, and in investment trends. Therefore, it is important to review your personal financial plan, its assumptions, and the conclusions drawn from it periodically to be sure it still meets your needs.

Financial Planning Is Not Precise

The results illustrated in this book are not indicative of every situation, and results will vary. The results of your plan cannot be precise. When you are planning over many years, small changes in assumptions create large differences in future results. As investment returns, inflation, and taxes differ from the projected assumptions, your actual results will vary (perhaps significantly) from those originally presented in the plan you created.

The investment rates of return used in your plan should be based on long-term historical average rates of return for a well-diversified portfolio of stocks and bonds. However, past performance is no guarantee of future results. Investment returns and principal value of an investment will fluctuate so that an investor's shares, when redeemed, may be worth more or less than their original cost and the values used in their plan.

No representation is being made that any strategy outlined in this book will, or is likely to, repeatedly achieve the same or similar results expressed in this book. The information herein is provided in this book is solely to educate on a variety of topics, including wealth planning, tax considerations, insurance, estate, divorce and special needs planning. All examples, illustrations, stories, and strategies are for general information purposes only. This book does not replace professional financial, tax, or legal advice.

Where appropriate the author and publisher encourage every reader to seek the advice of qualified financial, legal, and tax professional to assist in the creation and implementation of a comprehensive financial plan. Neither the author nor the publisher assumes any liability or responsibility for any errors or omissions and shall have neither liability nor responsibility to any person or entity with respect to damage caused or alleged to be caused directly or indirectly by the information contained in this book, audiobook, or corresponding workbook. Use at your own risk.